THEORY AND PRACTICE
Book 1 Collegiate Series

IROL WHITMORE BALSLEY, Ed.D.
Professor of Education
Texas Tech University

System Design and Research Consultant
EDWARD L. CHRISTENSEN, Ph.D.
Professor of Business Management
Brigham Young University

Shorthand Plates Written by **STANFORD D. DeMILLE**

R70

CINCINNATI   WEST CHICAGO, ILL.   DALLAS   PELHAM MANOR, N.Y.
BURLINGAME, CALIF.   BRIGHTON, ENGLAND

Copyright © 1974
by South-Western Publishing Co.
Cincinnati, Ohio

ALL RIGHTS RESERVED

The text of this publication, or any part thereof, may not
be reproduced or transmitted in any form or by any means,
electronic or mechanical, including photocopying, recording, storage in an information retrieval system, or otherwise,
without the prior written permission of the publisher.

ISBN: 0-538-18700-X

Library of Congress Catalog Card Number: 72-81798

1 2 3 4 5 6 7 H 0 9 8 7 6 5 4

Printed in the United States of America

PREFACE

Skill in manual shorthand transforms a "good" secretary into an "elite" secretary. With it she can record messages or data anywhere at any time—whether it be at an executive's desk, on an airliner, or at an archaeological site. She needs only a pen or pencil and paper; thus, she has maximum adaptability.

Personnel in the management ranks are usually the highest paid; therefore, maximizing their time is of paramount importance. If an executive has an "elite" secretary, he doesn't have to operate a machine (or even hold a phone) to dictate, to push buttons to recall what he has said or to alter what he has said, or to give complete directions as he dictates. He can concentrate fully on the message he wishes to convey or on the events of the day if he is working with his secretary on the daily planning activity. Sensitive material can be handled easily and quickly. He has auxiliary help right at hand if he needs it because the secretary is knowledgeable about the firm's business—she is not just a recording device. He can give directions for a myriad of activities and know they will be carried out because she jots down the salient points with a few shorthand strokes in her notebook.

Dictating and transcribing machines and machine shorthand systems have their place in the business world, but their use limitations and cost negate their supplanting manual shorthand with its adaptability and flexibility.

Hundreds of shorthand systems have been invented; few have survived. To be successful, a shorthand system must be easy to learn and to write. *Century 21* has achieved this goal by using (1) single symbols for sounds, (2) single direction for all symbols, and (3) dominant direction movement, which makes the construction of outlines for infrequent words easy and without decision pause. These characteristics also minimize decision pauses in transcription.

In this first volume of the Collegiate Series, emphasis is placed on the mastery of the theory of the system. The theory is presented in 27 of the first 33 lessons, a "breather" lesson occurring in Lessons 4, 8, 12, 16, 20, and 28.

Mastery of each principle is promoted through providing for application of that principle in three consecutive lessons.

Speedforms, shortened outlines for some of the most frequently used words, facilitate speed in writing. Each Speedform appears in five consecutive lessons as an aid to automatization.

Color is used as an aid to learning. Speedforms appear in color in the lessons in which they are introduced. Color highlights key outlines in various types of exercises, such as Word Selection, Spelling, and Phonetic Studies.

The student proceeds from the simple to the complex, starting with abundant plate notes and progressing to new dictation material with previews.

Extension of ability to take sustained dictation is insured through such devices as the short Sprint and the Dash (which gradually increases in length from 100 to 350 words).

Pretranscription training begins in Lesson 46 through exercises in punctuation, word differentiation, derivative development, and spelling.

A carefully planned program of dictation tests is provided. The vocabulary of each test is controlled through a computer record of all words introduced in each lesson. While the letters and memos in the tests are new material, the vocabulary has been previously introduced.

Supplementary material is included in the instructor's manual to give added flexibility to the instructor's planning.

Appreciation is expressed to the schools that used the system during the tryout period: Brigham Young University, University of Cincinnati, Fresno State University, and Cincinnati Technical College.

Manual shorthand skill, the most flexible and adaptable of recording methods, is a practical tool of communication that is an entree to the highest echelons of business. *Century 21* is for those who aspire to become "elite" secretaries in a minimum of time.

Irol W. Balsley

THEORY INDEX

PRIMARY

	Lesson
a	1-B
e	1-B
i	1-B
short i	17-E
o	1-B
u	1-B
diphthongs	
oi,oy	19-C
ou,ow	17-C
double syllables	
ia	32-B
io	32-B
iu	32-B
consonants	
b	9-C
d	3-E
f	3-C
g,j	11-D
h	11-B
k	3-B
l	2-D
m	10-C
n	3-D
p	10-D
r	1-E
s,z	1-B
t	1-D
v,w	2-C
y	24-C
digraphs	
ch	11-C
ng	15-C
sh,zh	7-B
th,Th	2-B

DERIVED

bends	Lesson
dm,dn	23-B
tm,tn	17-B
fr	10-B
gr,jr	15-B

DERIVED

	Lesson
nd,nt,nv	5-D
ld	22-F
blends	
dd,dt,td	18-C
mm,mn	13-D
nk	15-D
ellipses	
ya	24-C
ye	24-C
yi	24-C
word beginnings—joined	
al-	21-C
be-	9-C
com-	22-D
con-	22-C
de-	3-E
ex-	17-D
im-	32-C
in-	13-B
ind-,int-,inv-	5-D
per-,pur-	18-B
pre-	18-B
pro-	18-B
re-	3-D
sub-	27-B
un-	19-B
word beginnings—disjoined	
electr-	32-D
inter-,intr-	18-D
super,supr-	33-D
tran-,trans-	30-G
word endings—joined	
-ble	22-B
-ful	25-B
-gram	31-C
-graph	31-C
-ject	30-D
-ly	13-C
-ment	13-E
-sion,tion	7-C
-ther,-thor	19-D

DERIVED

word endings—disjoined	Lesson
-acle,-ical,-icle	24-B
-alogy,-ology	33-F
-bility	29-B
-casion,-cation	25-C
-cher,-ture	23-C
-ed	6-C
-er,-or (SFR, CF)	23-E
-ety,-ity	26-D
-hood,-ward	30-C
-ing	7-D
-ingly	33-C
-ings	25-E
-ive,-sive,-tive	26-B
-ous,-us	29-C
-sation,-zation	25-D
-scribe	27-C
-script	27-C
-ship	30-B
-titude,-titute,-tude	32-E
-tual	26-E
-ulate	31-D
compound elements	
electric	32-D
over	21-B
self	31-B
under	14-D
geographic elements	
-ville	32-F
-berg,-burg,-burgh	26-C
-field	33-E
-port	26-C
St.	26-C
New	24-E
specials	
yo	24-C
yu	24-C
look alike	
i	33-B

Index

SPEEDFORMS INDEX

SF	Lesson	SF	Lesson	SF	Lesson	SF	Lesson
a	1	correspondence	6	improve	15	request	3
able	1	count	6	in	3	require	5
about	9	custom	6	individual	5	respect	15
accept	3	deliver	3	industry	5	response	5
accord	6	department	11	information	10	result	5
active	18	develop	6	inspect	15	return	1
activity	18	difficult	6	instruct	13	satisfactory	1
administer	13	direct	3	interest	18	satisfy	1
advance	6	discuss	3	invitation	5	secretary	3
advantage	14	distinct	15	invite	5	send	3
advertise	2	distinguish	15	is	1	serve	2
advice	2	distribute	13	issue	7	shall	7
advise	2	down	9	it	1	ship	7
affect	3	economic	18	just	11	short	7
after	3	economy	18	letter	2	situate	14
agriculture	15	educate	11	manufacture	13	situation	14
am	10	effect	3	material	10	special	13
amount	10	elect	9	merchandise	11	specific	15
an	1	employ	15	more	10	specify	15
and	5	enclose	5	mortgage	13	stand	17
announce	17	enough	9	must	10	state	1
anxious	15	envelope	5	necessary	3	success	3
any	3	equip	14	newspaper	15	suggest	11
appreciate	10	establish	14	next	9	sure	7
approximate	15	event	5	not	3	than	3
are	1	ever	2	notice	9	thank	14
as	1	expect	17	number	10	that	2
associate	1	expense	17	of	2	the	2
at	1	experience	17	one	3	their	2
attention	17	fact	3	opportunity	14	them	10
be	9	figure	18	order	3	then	3
been	9	form	10	organization	11	there	2
business	9	found	9	organize	11	thing	18
by	9	from	10	our	1	think	14
can	3	go	11	out	17	throughout	17
certificate	9	good	11	part	11	time	17
certify	9	govern	11	particular	15	value	9
chairman	11	graduate	15	please	10	very	2
change	11	great	15	present	18	want	5
committee	10	ground	15	probable	18	was	2
company	10	has	11	problem	18	well	2
condition	3	have	2	product	18	what	2
consider	6	he	1	prompt	18	when	5
construct	6	his	1	provide	18	where	2
contact	9	hope	10	public	10	which	11
contain	17	hospital	15	publish	10	while	2
contract	9	hour	1	quality	3	why	2
contribute	13	how	17	quantity	6	will	2
control	9	if	3	question	3	with	2
convenience	5	immediate	14	receive	1	won	3
convenient	5	immediately	14	record	3	work	3
convention	9	importance	14	regard	15	worth	2
correspond	6	important	14	regular	11	would	3
				report	14	your	1

Index

GENERAL INDEX

Abbreviations, 56, 218
Adapt, adept, adopt, 184
Add, ad, 167
Addition, edition, 206
Advice, advise, 169
Affect, effect, 137
All ready, already, 193
Aloud, allowed, 209
Alter, altar, 164
Alternate, alternate, 194
Appropriate, appropriate, 194
Assent, ascent, 167
Assistance, assistants, 206
Bade, bad, 212
Bass, base, 197
Beach, beech, 172
Bear, bare, 190
Beside, besides, 157
Blue, blew, bleu, 175
Borne, born, 181
Bow, bough, 209
Break, brake, 164
Breath, breathe, 203
Canvas, canvass, 172
Capital, capitol, 154
Capitalization, 2
Cents, sense, 205
Cite, sight, site, 178
Clothe, cloth, 206
Colonel, kernel, 181
Complementary, complimentary, 175
Compound words, 8
Consonant shapes, 2
Contracted forms, 38
Contractions, 82
Core, corps, 196
Correspondence forms, 38
Council, counsel, 166
Dash, 34
Daze, days, 184
Deceased, diseased, 181
Decent, descent, 209
Derivative development, 164, 167, 170, 172, 176, 179, 182, 184, 187, 190, 194, 197, 200, 203, 206, 209, 212, 216, 218
Desolate, desolate, 215
Dessert, desert, 203
Device, devise, 151
Dominant direction, 2
Duplicate, duplicate, 197
End of letter marks, 27
Eraser, erasure, 181
Fare, fair, 167
Farther, further, 160

Fractions, 104
Guarantee, guaranty, 148
Guessed, guest, 175
Heard, herd, 169
Heir, air, 190
Hyphen, 21
Idle, Idol, 203
Inclined, inclined, 215
Interstate, intrastate, 187
It's, its, 146
Kiln, kill, 190
Knight, night, 169
Know, no, 169
Later, latter, 143
Leased, least, 172
Led, lead, 200
Loose, lose, 197
Marshal, martial, 178
Mean, mein, 200
Meat, meet, 187
Meddle, medal, 187
Miner, minor, 172
Minute, minute, 197
Money terms, 56
Moral, morale, 199
Mourning, morning, 164
Notebook, handling of, 13
Numbers, 6
Paragraph indication, 20
Pare, pear, 164
Passed, past, 202
Patience, patients, 206
Peer, pier, 200
Perfect, perfect, 194
Period, 2
Phrasing, 2
Phonetic studies, 164, 167, 169, 172, 175, 178, 181, 187, 190, 193, 197, 200, 203, 206, 209, 212, 215
Piece, peace, 187
Plane, plain, 184
Possessive form, 4
Pray, prey, 187
Principal, principle, 190
Prophet, profit, 179
Pull, pool, 206
Punctuation rules, 133, 136, 139, 142, 145, 148, 151, 154, 157, 160, 163, 166, 168, 171, 174, 177, 180, 183, 186, 189, 192, 196, 199, 202, 205
Question mark, 45
Quotation marks, 45
Raze, raise, 209

Reigning, raining, 215
Residents, residence, 169
Rode, road, 181
Roll, role, 172
Roots, routes, 203
Sales, sails, 200
Sealing, ceiling, 175
Seam, seem, 203
See, sea, 190
Seen, scene, 181
Seize, cease, 167
Separate, separate, 193
Serge, surge, 212
Sew, sow, 212
Sewer, sower, 197
Slay, sleigh, 212
Sole, soul, 187
Spelling demons, 134, 137, 140, 143, 146, 149, 152, 155, 158, 160, 163, 167, 169, 172, 175, 178, 181, 184, 187, 190, 193, 196, 200, 203, 206, 209, 212, 215, 218
Spelling rules, 220, 225, 229, 234, 240
Stake, steak, 178
Stationary, stationery, 163
Steal, steel, 164
Straight, strait, 175
Study suggestions, 13
Suspect, suspect, 193
Teemed, teamed, 197
Their, there, 140
Threw, through, 184
Thrown, throne, 179
Time of day, 56
To, too, two, 133
U written after n, 11
Vain, vane, 178
Veil, vale, 184
Vowel shapes, 2
Waist, waste, 172
Waive, wave, 200
Weak, week, 175
Whole, hole, 167
"Why" of shorthand phonetic spelling, 1
Word division rules, 137, 141, 143
Word selection, 133, 137, 140, 143, 146, 148, 151, 154, 157, 160, 163, 166, 169, 172, 175, 178, 181, 184, 187, 190, 193, 196, 199, 202, 205
Wrapping, rapping, 190
Write, *right, rite,* 169
Writing rules, 9
Wrote, rote, 209

Shorthand
AN EXCITING TOOL OF COMMUNICATION

1-A. THE "WHY" OF SHORTHAND

Everyone Communicates. Everyone is involved in communication every day; sometimes it is oral and sometimes it is written. Shorthand is a tool by which the oral communication can be recorded. Someone who wishes to prepare a written communication quickly can do so by dictating his message to a shorthand writer who uses this tool. The writer can make notes and prepare a transcript, thus enabling the dictator to concentrate on his thoughts without becoming involved with the mechanics of manual or machine recording.

Shorthand is most often thought of as the tool of a stenographer or secretary in an office, but it is helpful to others—the buyer at a fashion show making notes, the newspaper reporter jotting down salient points of an interview, the homemaker preparing a grocery list or noting directions given in a TV program. Since the most frequent use of shorthand is in the business office, the material in this book will be focused primarily on recording for the business communications area.

Oral Communication Is Too Rapid for Longhand Recording. When people converse with each other or when they speak formally before a group, their rate of speech is much too rapid to be recorded in longhand. Frequently a listener would like to jot down either every word that is spoken or at least the gist of the message, but longhand is too slow. By using symbols for sounds, either type of recording is possible.

Legible longhand can be written at a maximum of about 35 words a minute; shorthand can be written three or four times that fast— even faster by expert shorthand writers. When we realize that people normally speak in excess of 150 words a minute and, when excited or in a hurry, may reach over 300 words a minute, the need for a means of recording rapidly is obvious.

Dictation Systems May Vary. A dictator may dictate to (a) a writer of manual shorthand, (b) a writer of machine shorthand, or (c) a machine that records on a belt, disc, or tape. Each method is useful for certain recording situations. Regardless of the method, the dictator can minimize dictation time by having organized his thoughts before dictation begins and also by permitting no interruptions by phone or personal calls during dictation.

Recording by a manual shorthand writer is especially suited to the executive because of (a) the feasibility of interspersing dictation with other matters during the executive-secretary daily planning session, (b) the confidential nature of much of the dictation, and (c) the ease of dictating without having to operate mechanical equipment.

A Symbol System Is Based on Phonetic Spellings. A symbol system of shorthand is one in which speech sounds are written by using certain marks or strokes for various sounds. Phonetic spelling tells you that the sound of *age* is āj; of *ice*, īs; of *rule*, rūl. Notice that the sound of *c* in *ice* is *s*; therefore, *ice* is written by combining the symbols for *i* and *s*. In the word *rule*, the *e* is not pronounced (neither was it in *ice*), so in shorthand we combine into one outline the symbols for *r*, *u*, and *l*, omitting the *e*.

The upside down e (ə) represents the phonetic schwa or neutral vowel which is not written in shorthand. Can you recognize the longhand words for the following?

sīt	fū	pīn	ūs	bōt
sītē	füd	pin	us	būt
	pri pãr		kəmūnətē	
	līəbilətē		səb mit	

You are about to begin the acquisition of one of the most useful tools in recording and communicating. Each lesson builds on the foundation of the preceding one, so make adequate preparation *every* day. If you **do**, learning shorthand will be a most satisfying experience in which you acquire an exciting tool of communication!

80-D. THEORY REVIEW

1-B. SHORTHAND ALPHABET

Sound(s) of	Shorthand Stroke(s)	Longhand Word(s)
ā		
ē		
ū		you
s, z		

Think *sound*!

LEARNING HINTS. Note that a vowel is a circle or half a circle; a consonant is a straight stroke, a curved stroke, or a dot.

Most of the shorthand outlines in the system are written in the *dominant* ( ) direction of longhand, making it easy to learn to write.

Some words are expressed by a single stroke, as in *you*; others, by combining strokes in the order in which the sounds are uttered in pronouncing the word, as in:

sā   say   sē   see (sea)

A period is:

Read these sentences:
               You see.   You say.

For faster writing and reading, we can combine these outlines:

This combining of outlines is *phrasing*. Phrase only as directed.

Sound(s) of	Shorthand Stroke(s)	Longhand Word(s)
ī		I (eye)
ō		owe (oh)

Read these sentences:

Sound(s) of	Shorthand Stroke(s)	Longhand Word(s)
sēz		seize (sees)
sō		so (sew, sow)
sū		Sue

Capitalization is indicated by a short, forward straight line under the last stroke of the word to be capitalized.

To facilitate the reading of shorthand notes in the early lessons, each punctuation mark within a sentence will be given and encircled to make recognition easy.

Try these sentences:

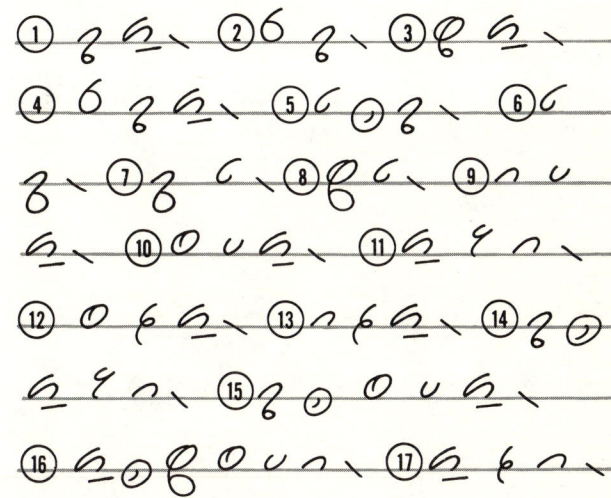

1-C. SPEEDFORMS

Speedforms are short outlines which should be written with unusual speed and ease. For this reason, they are to be memorized.

LESSON 1

Speedforms and Speedform related words will appear in color for easy recognition in their presentation lesson and in recaps of that lesson. If they are phrased with other words, the entire outline will appear in color.

Speedform	Longhand Word(s)
.	a, an
o	able
(	as, his, is
ℓ	associate
o	he
∩	your

▷ **LEARNING HINT.** *You* and *your* are expressed by the same symbol.

A question mark is:

New phrases: as you see, as you say, he is, is your, he sees

New word: use

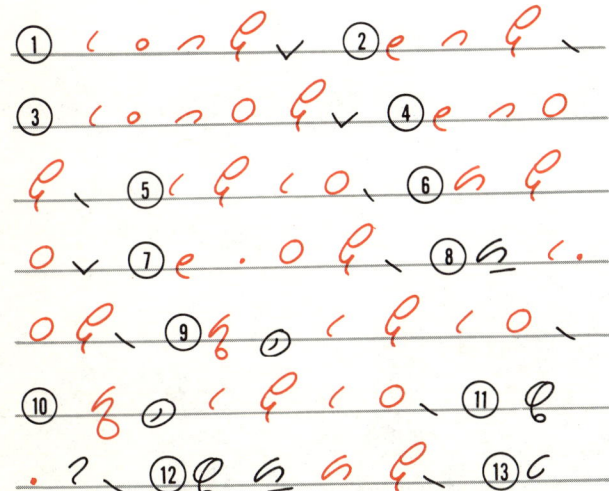

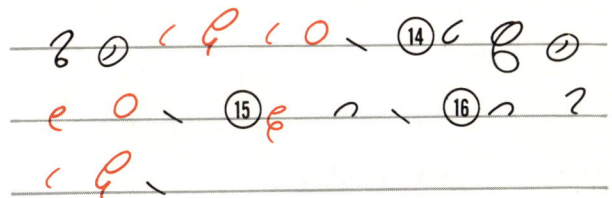

▷ **LEARNING HINT.** Notice that shorthand notebook paper is set up in two columns to save arm movement for the shorthand writer. He writes down the first column before going to the second one. Therefore, you will read the left-hand column before reading the right-hand column.

● **1-D. SHORTHAND ALPHABET**

Sound(s) of	Shorthand Stroke(s)	Longhand Word(s)
t	╱	
āt	⌒	ate
sēts	↻	seats
sīt	↻	sight site (cite)
tīz	ℛ	ties
tü	⌒	to, too, two

▶ **NOTE:** The *t* is a short, slanting straight stroke written upward.

New phrase: to use

LESSON 1 **Page 3**

LESSON 80

80-A. PHRASE-WRITING MASTERY

80-B. PREVIEWED NEW DICTATION

Take from dictation material that you previewed in 79-D-4.

80-C. AUTOMATIZATION OF FREQUENTLY USED WORDS

LESSON 80

Page 244

Using the *t* stroke, you can write some more of the most frequently used words as Speedforms.

Speedform	Longhand Word(s)
╱	*at, it*
6	*satisfactory, satisfy*
⋎	*state*

New phrases: ╱ it is   ⋎ is it

⌒ to you (to your)

▶ **LEARNING HINT.** Sometimes the outline for a phrase is written with the same strokes as the outline for a single word as in *is it* and *state*. The first outline in sentences 6, 8, and 9 is the phrase *is it*. The context of the sentence will indicate the proper usage.

1-E. SHORTHAND ALPHABET

Sound(s) of	Shorthand Stroke(s)	Longhand Word(s)
r	⌒	
rāz	ℯ	*raise*
rāt	⌒	*rate*
rīt	⌒	*right, write (rite)*
stôr	⌒	*store*

▶ **NOTE:** The *r* is a short curved stroke written forward.

▶ **LEARNING HINT.** The possessive form can be recognized through context, as in: ℯ *associate's.*

Speedform	Longhand Word(s)
⌒	*are, hour, our*
6	*receive*
ℯ	*return*

New phrases:

New word: 6 *easy*

LESSON 1   **Page 4**

79-D-4. VOCABULARY PREVIEW OF NEW MATERIAL

athletic, advanced, family, trampolines, we would like, season, prior, Christmas, destination, quantity, policy

NOTE: *To* is written ⌒ ; but, when *to* is followed by a downstroke, only the *t* needs to be written. Compare *to see* and *to say* with *to receive*.

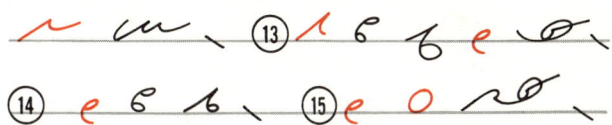

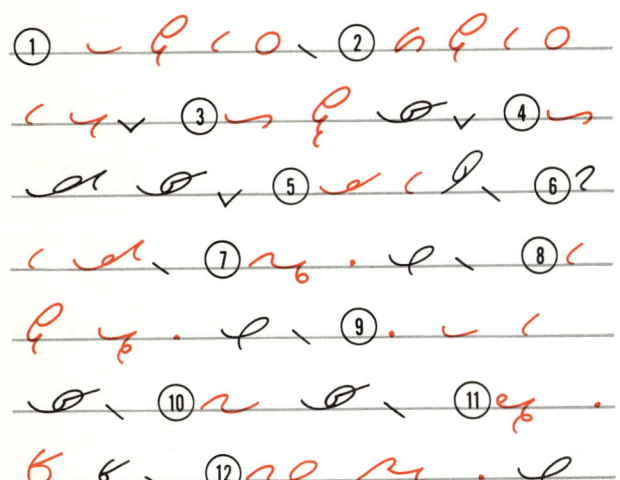

1-F. PREPARATION FOR LESSON 2

Before beginning Lesson 2, practice reading the sentences in the exercises in Lesson 1 until you can read them fluently. If you cannot recall the word for a black outline, spell it aloud; for an outline in color, turn back to the exercise that identifies it as a Speedform.

Think *sound*! What are the longhand words for the following phonetic spellings?

| *thēz* | *sāl* | *vōt* | *thrē* | *trā* | *wīz* |
| *sāv* | *lā* | *thrü* | *lāt* | *rül* | *wē* |

LESSON 2

2-A. RECAP OF LESSON 1

New phrase: ╱ to satisfy

New word: ⌒ try

2-B. SHORTHAND ALPHABET

Sound(s) of	Shorthand Stroke(s)	Longhand Word(s)
th	↗	
thēz	⌒	these
thā	⌒	they
thrü	⌢	through (threw)

NOTE: The *th* is a short, upward curved stroke.

New phrase: ⌒ they are

New words: ⌒ tires   ⌒ tray

LESSON 2 **Page 5**

LESSON 79

▶ **NOTE:** In writing shorthand, numbers above 2 are always written in Arabic numerals.

Speedform		Longhand Word(s)
		that
		the
		their, there

New phrases: ⟿ that the   ⟿ at the   ⟿ there are   ⟿ they receive   ⟿ that is   ⟿ is that

New words: ⟿ Ray   ⟿ true

2-C. SHORTHAND ALPHABET

Sound(s) of	Shorthand Stroke(s)	Longhand Word(s)
v, w		
sāv		save
vōt		vote
wāt		wait (weight)
wē		we
wīz		wise

▶ **NOTE:** The *v, w* is a short curved stroke, written in the dominant direction.

New phrases: ⟿ we are   ⟿ to save

Speedform		Longhand Word(s)
		advice, advise
		have, with

LESSON 2 — **Page 6**

(b) *re* as a prefix may need to be followed by a hyphen if the word could have two meanings (such as *recover* and *re-cover*); and (c) a prefix preceding a proper noun is separated from that noun by a hyphen.

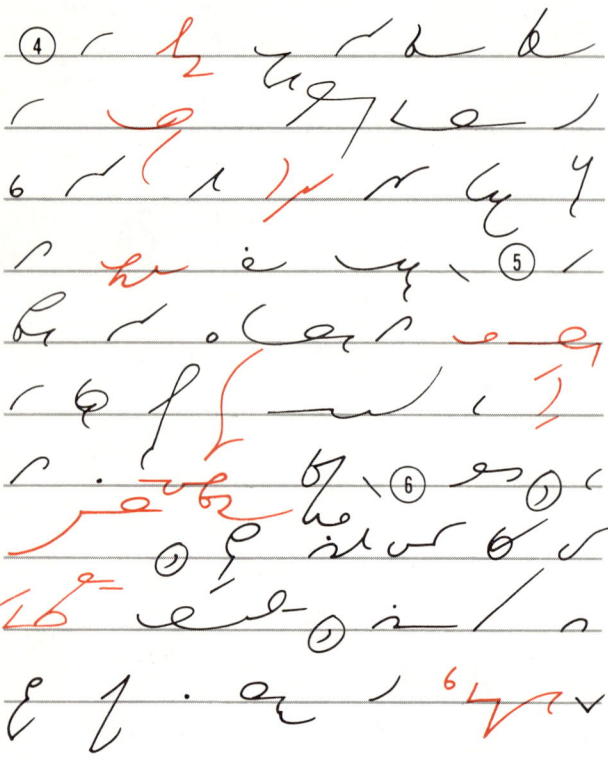

Rule 10. If a word ending begins with a vowel, do not double the final consonant of the root word under any of these circumstances: (a) if the accent falls on any syllable other than the last one; (b) if the word ending consists of more than one consonant; (c) if the word ending is a single consonant preceded by more than one vowel.

NOTE: Some commonly used exceptions are *cancellation* and *questionnaire*.

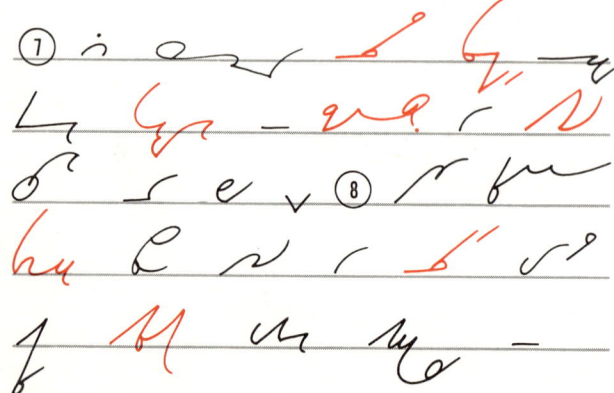

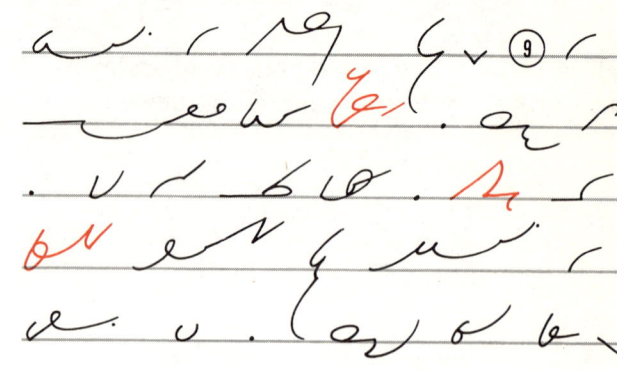

79-D-2. THEORY REVIEW

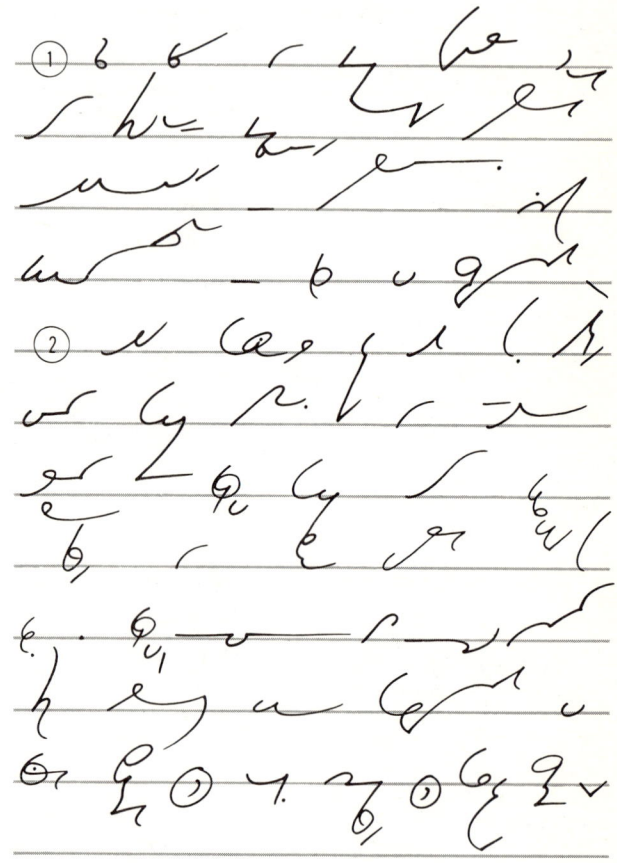

79-D-3. OFFICE-STYLE NOTES

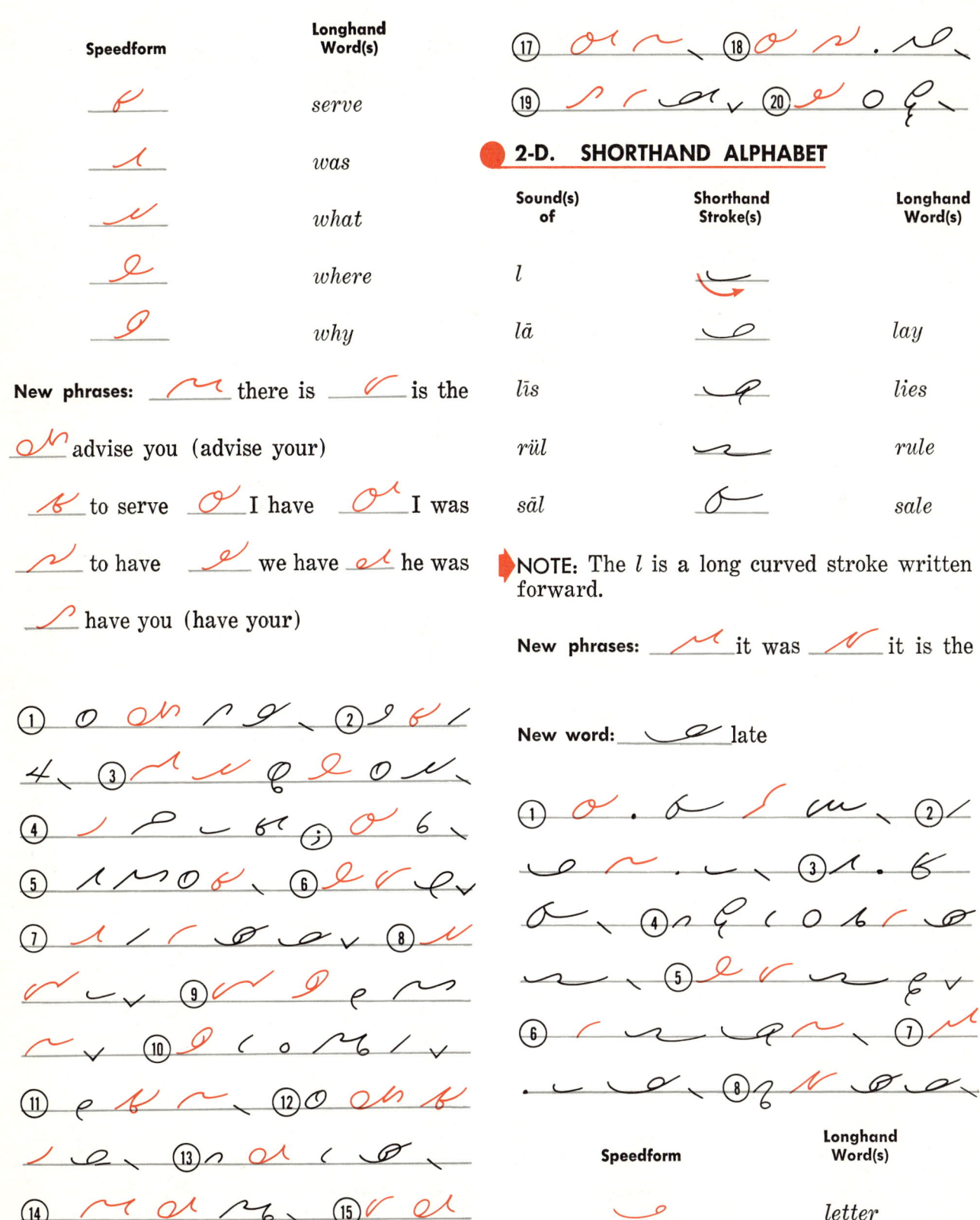

79-D. PREPARATION FOR LESSON 80

Follow the same procedures as for the preceding lessons.

79-D-1. SPELLING RULES

Rule 8. If a word ending begins with a vowel, double the final consonant of the root word when that final consonant is single and is preceded by a vowel and the word is one syllable or is accented on the last syllable.

> NOTE: There are some consonants that are exceptions, such as *c*, *w*, and *j*, and some commonly used words that are exceptions, such as *reference*, *preference*, and *transferable*. Consult the dictionary when in doubt.

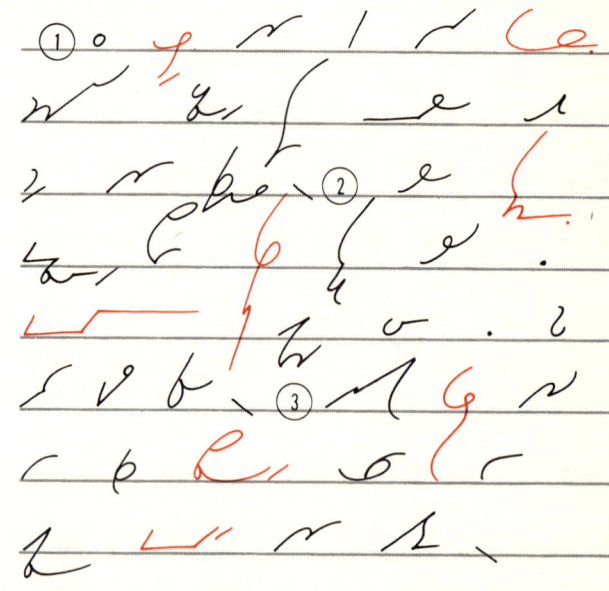

Rule 9. If the first element of a compound word is a prefix or the last element is a suffix, the compound is usually written as one word. Some exceptions are: (a) *self* as a prefix is nearly always followed by a hyphen;

LESSON 79   Page 240

Additional Speedforms using the v, w stroke:

	advertise
	ever
	very
	while
	worth

The o stroke is used for the Speedform:

	of

New phrases: I will — of the — to the — will you (will your) — of his — we will — you will — I will receive — you will see — I will have — he will have

New word: every

▶ **LEARNING HINT.** Many compound words are written in shorthand by simply combining the outlines for the single words that form the compound as:

worthwhile

▶ **NOTE:** The plural of *letters* is written to distinguish it from *lease*.

2-E. PREPARATION FOR LESSON 3

Before starting Lesson 3, practice reading the sentences in Lesson 2 until you can read at no less than 60 words a minute.

Except for Speedforms, the words you have learned so far have had the "long" vowel sounds as in *rate*, *see*, *you*, and *I*. In Lesson 3 you will be encountering shorthand outlines for words in which other sounds of the vowels occur.

Study the following rules for writing or omitting various vowel sounds. Spell the words by sound and then say each word so that you will recognize it the next time you see it.

LESSON 2 — Page 8

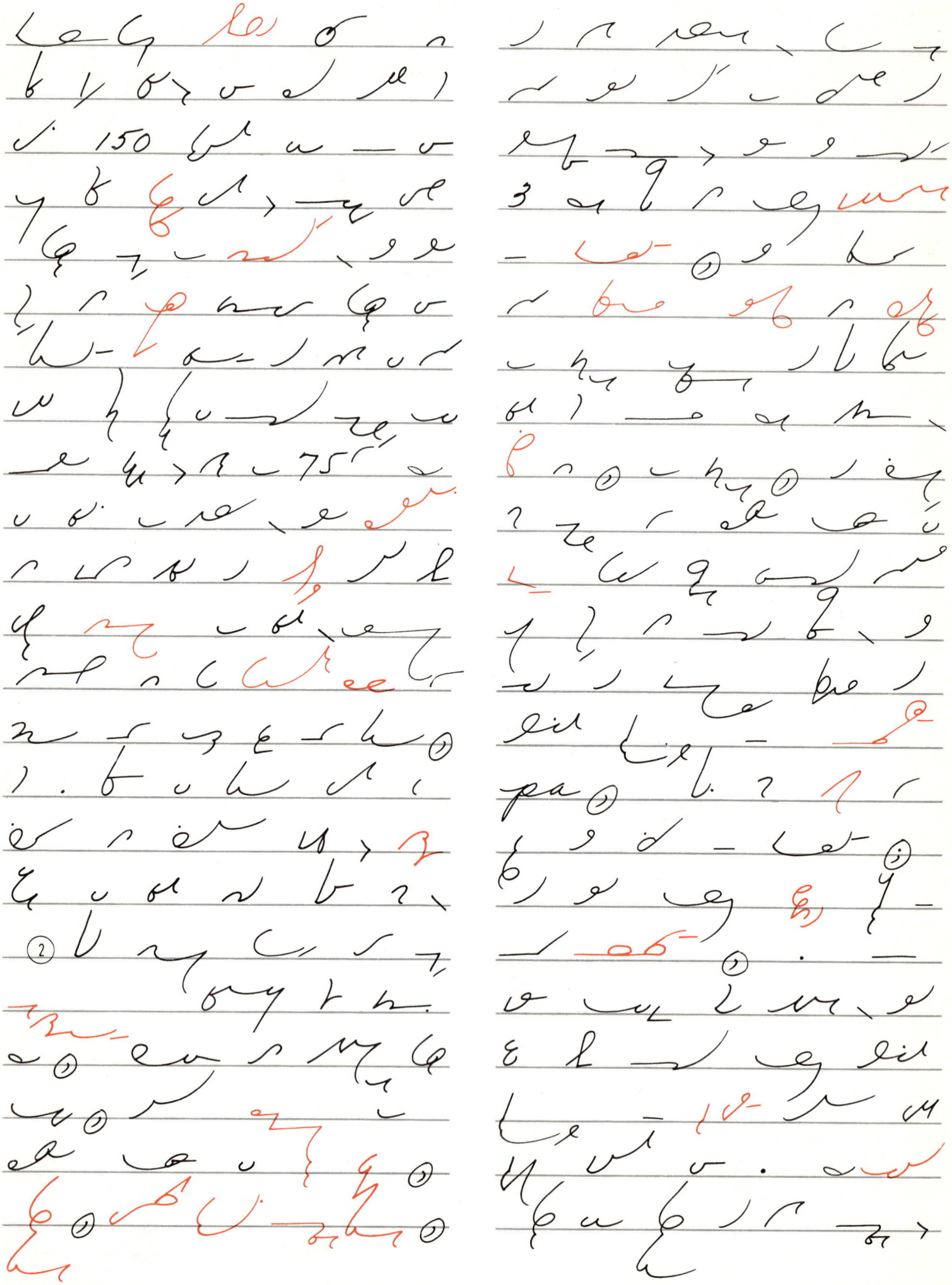

1. All basic and neutral sounds of vowels are written at the beginnings and ends of words. For example:

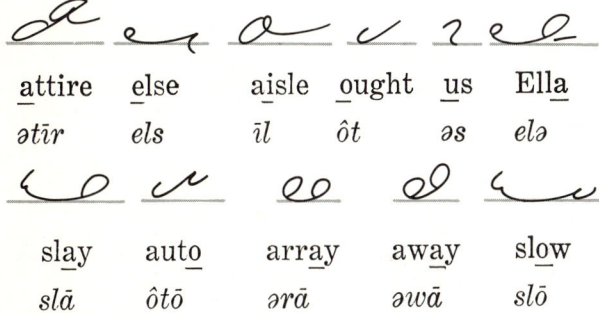

attire	else	aisle	ought	us	Ella
ətīr	els	īl	ôt	əs	elə
slay	auto	array	away	slow	
slā	ôtō	ərā	əwā	slō	

2. Within the body of a word, all basic sounds of *a, e, o, u* are written. For example:

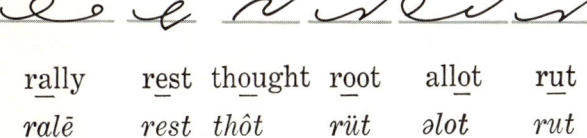

rally	rest	thought	root	allot	rut
ralē	rest	thôt	rüt	əlot	rut

3. Within the body of a word, the short sound of *i* is not written (the long sound *is* written). For example:

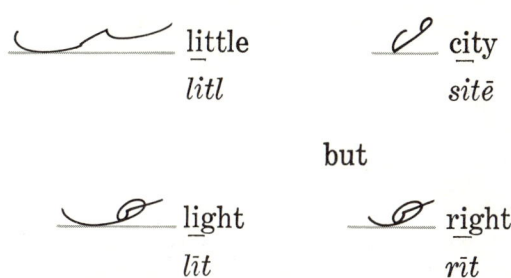

	little		city
	litl		sitē

but

	light		right
	līt		rīt

4. Within the body of a word, the unstressed (i.e., neutral or schwa) vowel is not written. For example:

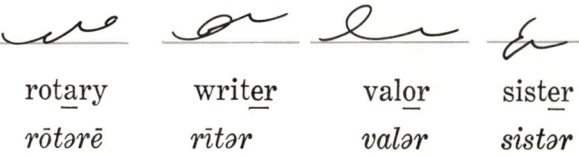

rotary	writer	valor	sister
rōtərē	rītər	valər	sistər

LESSON 3

3-A. RECAP OF LESSONS 1 and 2

New phrases: we will receive

at that

New word:  service

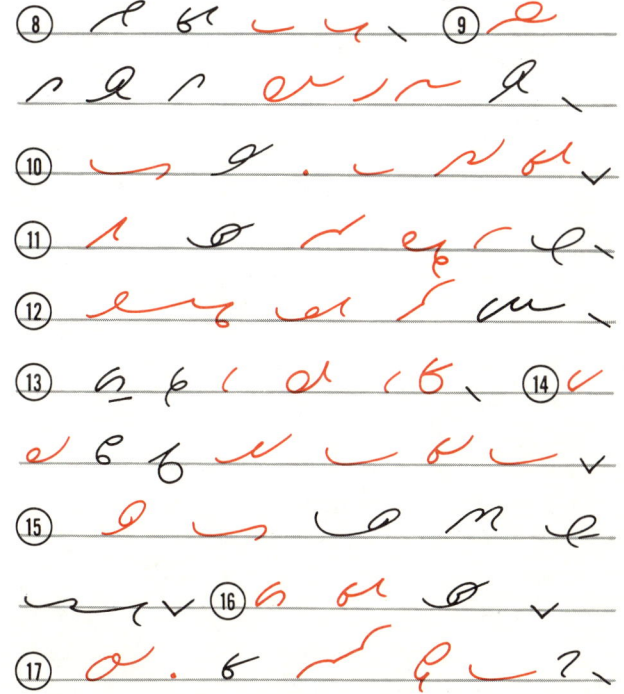

LESSON 3

Page 9

LESSON 79

● **79-A. PHRASE-WRITING MASTERY**

● **79-B. PREVIEWED NEW DICTATION**

Your teacher will dictate to you new material previewed in 78-D-4.

● **79-C. AUTOMATIZATION OF FREQUENTLY USED WORDS**

LESSON 79

Page 238

3-B. SHORTHAND ALPHABET

Sound(s) of	Shorthand Stroke(s)	Longhand Word(s)
k		
kär (kâr)		car (care)
kās		case
kēz		keys
līk		like
tāk		take

NOTE: The *k* is a short straight stroke written downward and is the size of the *s* stroke.

New phrases: you have — to take — with the — I like — he likes — of your (of you)

New words: Kate — this

Speedform	Longhand Word(s)
	can
	quality
	question
	request
	secretary
	work

Additional Speedform: success

New phrases: I can — of our — can you (can your) — I can see — you can — you like — that will — we can see

LESSON 3 — Page 10

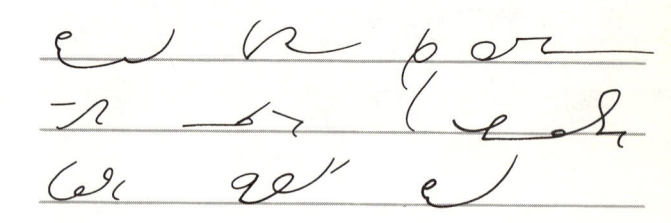

eligible, professional, economic, geography finance, administration, international, demands, excellent, potential, capability, advancement, interviews, meetings, recommendations, previous, acquainted, exchange

Benson, outing, interrupted, disrupted, catalytic, warehouse, phenomenal, somewhat, slowness, upsets, availability, flexibility, substitutions

78-D-4. VOCABULARY PREVIEW OF NEW MATERIAL

accumulated, recorded, library, units, behalf, access, executives, regrouping, classification, system, traffic, export-import, otherwise, searching, extension, teacher, audio-visual, designate, runner, quote, comments, presentation, literature, supplemental, educational, dividend (CF), shares, enthusiasm (CF), kindly, urgent

LESSON 78 Page 237

3-C. SHORTHAND ALPHABET

Sound(s) of	Shorthand Stroke(s)	Longhand Word(s)
f	∕	
fēl	↙	feel
fū	↙	few
fīlz	↙	files

▶ NOTE: The *f* is a middle-sized straight stroke written downward.

New phrases: I feel   he will see   that are (that hour, that our)

Speedform	Longhand Word(s)
	affect, after
	effect
	fact, if

New phrases: after the   if you can   if you like   it will have   I will see   I will say   I can say

New words: race   little

Add another Speedform: accept

3-D. SHORTHAND ALPHABET

Sound(s) of	Shorthand Stroke(s)	Longhand Word(s)
n	→	
an		Ann
fīn		fine
nū		knew, new
nō		know (no)

▶ NOTE: The *n* is a short straight stroke written forward; the *u* is written on its side after *n* to increase speed, as in   .

New phrases: I know   I knew

New word: tell

LESSON 3   Page 11

Speedform	Longhand Word(s)
	any
	in, not
	necessary
	one, won
	send
	than, then

New phrases: ⌒ you know ⌒ in that ⌒ it is not ⌒ in this ⌒ to send ⌒ we will have ⌒ I will not ⌒ in the

New words: ⌒ easier ⌒ even ⌒ thought ⌒ on

① ② ③ ④ ⑤ ⑥

New phrases: ⌒ is not ⌒ than the ⌒ we can ⌒ on your (on you) ⌒ on the ⌒ on our ⌒ in our ⌒ send the

New words: ⌒ reserve ⌒ list

NOTE: Word beginnings having the sounds of *re-* and *ri-* are written ⌒ .

① ② ③ ④ ⑤ ⑥ ⑦

3-E. SHORTHAND ALPHABET

Sound(s) of	Shorthand Stroke(s)	Longhand Word(s)
d		
dāz		days (daze)
dü		do, due
dolərz		dollars
nēd		need

NOTE: The *d* is a long slanting stroke written upward. The sound of the word beginning *de-* (di) is also expressed by the *d* stroke. For example:

decrease   decline   delay   desire

New phrases: ⌒ do not ⌒ he can have

New words: ⌒ or ⌒ way (weigh)

① ② ③ ④

LESSON 3   **Page 12**

Rule 7. Words ending in a double consonant usually retain both consonants when the ending is added.

78-D-2. THEORY REVIEW

78-D-3. OFFICE-STYLE NOTES

LESSON 78 Page 235

Speedform	Longhand Word(s)
	condition
	deliver
	direct
	discuss
	order
	record
	would

New phrases: if you would like, I cannot, I would like, do you (do your), this is, send our, he would like

New word: city

3-F. STUDY SUGGESTIONS

1. Follow these suggestions for writing shorthand.

a. Use a good pen from which the ink flows freely. It should not be necessary to press down as you would with an ordinary pencil. Grasp the pen lightly so that you will be able to take dictation for one, two, or even three hours without feeling undue fatigue.

b. Always have at least two writing instruments with you. If one suddenly fails to function, you can quickly pick up the other and continue to write without losing any dictation.

c. If you do not know an outline for a dictated word, write as far as you do know and go on. The sense of the sentence may help you recall what you were trying to record.

d. Once you have a clear mental picture of the outline, execute it quickly; avoid drawing it.

e. When you write an incorrect outline, don't erase it. Just strike a line through it and write the outline correctly as shown below:

LESSON 3

78-D. PREPARATION FOR LESSON 79

Continue the same study pattern that you have used for previous lessons.

78-D-1. SPELLING RULES

Rule 6. If a noun ends in *y* preceded by a consonant, the plural is formed by changing the *y* to *i* and adding *es*. If the noun ends in *y* preceded by a vowel, the plural is formed by adding *s* to the singular.

NOTE: If the word is a proper noun ending in *y*, always add *s* to the singular form.

LESSON 78 — Page 234

2. Suggestions for handling the notebook efficiently for transcribing:

   a. Date your notebook daily. If you start each day's dictation on a clean sheet, you can place the date at the bottom of the page. This position makes finding a particular day's dictation easy; however, if you start the day's dictation on a partially used page, place the date immediately above the new dictation.

   b. Keep a rubber band around the pages containing "old" notes to facilitate turning to current dictation.

   c. Cancel the notes for each transcript as soon as you finish transcribing, as shown below; this will remove doubts about whether or not you did transcribe certain notes.

   d. As you read your notes, think of the *sense* of each sentence. If you do, you may be able to read outlines written incorrectly.

   e. Use your shorthand often. Take notes for other classes or try recording radio and TV programs.

3. Homework properly done serves two purposes: (a) it expands your shorthand vocabulary, i.e., the number of outlines you can write; and (b) it increases your speed in recalling outlines for words that are dictated, thus raising your notetaking rate. The following comments about homework will offer effective study techniques.

   a. Be able to read each letter smoothly before trying to write it.

   b. In practicing outlines in a word list, write each outline three consecutive times in your notebook, saying it as you write without looking in your book. Try the second outline; then, the third, etc.

   c. In practicing continuity material, read a "thought phrase," i.e., as many outlines as you can retain in your mind; then write it in your notebook two or three consecutive times, saying the words as you write. This procedure is called "double thought" phrase writing. DO NOT LOOK IN THE BOOK AS YOU WRITE. For example, if the letter reads, "He will return to the store to receive the letter. . .," the first "thought phrase" you pick might be "He will return." Write that phrase two or three times, saying it as you write. Then glance at the shorthand notes in the textbook to pick up the next phrase, "to the store." Write that phrase two or three times, saying it as you write WITHOUT LOOKING AT THE TEXTBOOK.

Your notes might look like this:

   d. Another effective procedure is to read a letter over and over until you can read it smoothly; write three consecutive times any outline that you cannot recall readily. Next, write the letter from the printed transcript. Check against the plate and then practice any outlines written incorrectly.

   e. Never write longhand in the shorthand plate material; this practice will deter rather than help.

3-G. PREPARATION FOR LESSON 4

1. Practice reading the plates in Lesson 3 until you can read them smoothly.

2. If your teacher so directs, write the sentences in 3-A in "double thought" phrases.

3. In Lesson 4 you will be writing shorthand for sentences that contain words for which you have already learned the shorthand outlines.

Shorthand is a device for recording more rapidly than can be done in longhand. Since speed is the goal of shorthand, concentrate on writing rapidly. Precision will come later.

LESSON 78

LESSON 4

4-A. NOTETAKING CONCENTRATION (LESSON 1)

In Lesson 3 you were introduced to writing shorthand; in this lesson you will have opportunity to practice writing sentences that contain words you have already learned.

These Notetaking Concentration lessons contain only review material; therefore, the use of a second color in the shorthand plates is not necessary.

Read a sentence; then try writing it without looking in the textbook. Check for correctness; then try again. Write as rapidly as you can. Avoid drawing the outlines.

[Shorthand exercises 1–25]

[Shorthand exercises 26–41]

4-B. NOTETAKING CONCENTRATION (LESSONS 1-2)

[Shorthand exercises 1–14]

LESSON 4 — **Page 15**

dinner, cafeteria, facilities, lunch, nemesis, juke, popular, considerably, function, welcome, campus, panel, events, family, acquaintances, outstanding, south

77-D-4. VOCABULARY PREVIEW OF NEW MATERIAL

regional, capabilities, ovation, evening, intensify, overhaul, solid, endorsement, treasury, terminal, recalling

LESSON 78

78-A. PHRASE-WRITING MASTERY

78-B. PREVIEWED NEW DICTATION

Take from dictation material that you previewed in 77-D-4.

78-C. AUTOMATIZATION OF FREQUENTLY USED WORDS

4-C. NOTETAKING CONCENTRATION
(LESSONS 1-3)

4-D. PREPARATION FOR LESSON 5

Time yourself on reading the sentences in 4-A, 4-B, and 4-C. Try to read them without hesitation.

Write each sentence in 4-C in "double thought" phrases. Get the sentence in mind and then write it in your notebook without looking in the textbook.

LESSON 5

5-A. RECAP OF LESSON 1

New word: ⌒ size

5-B. RECAP OF LESSONS 1 AND 2

New phrase: they have

New words: lot   those

5-C. RECAP OF LESSONS 1-3

New phrases: if the   if it is   affect the   it will not

New words: office   own   final   several   desk   ready   soon

Rule 5. The possessive of regular plurals is formed by adding an apostrophe after the *s*; of irregular plurals, by adding an apostrophe followed by an *s*. The possessive form of personal pronouns does not require an apostrophe.

77-D-2. THEORY REVIEW

77-D-3. OFFICE-STYLE NOTES

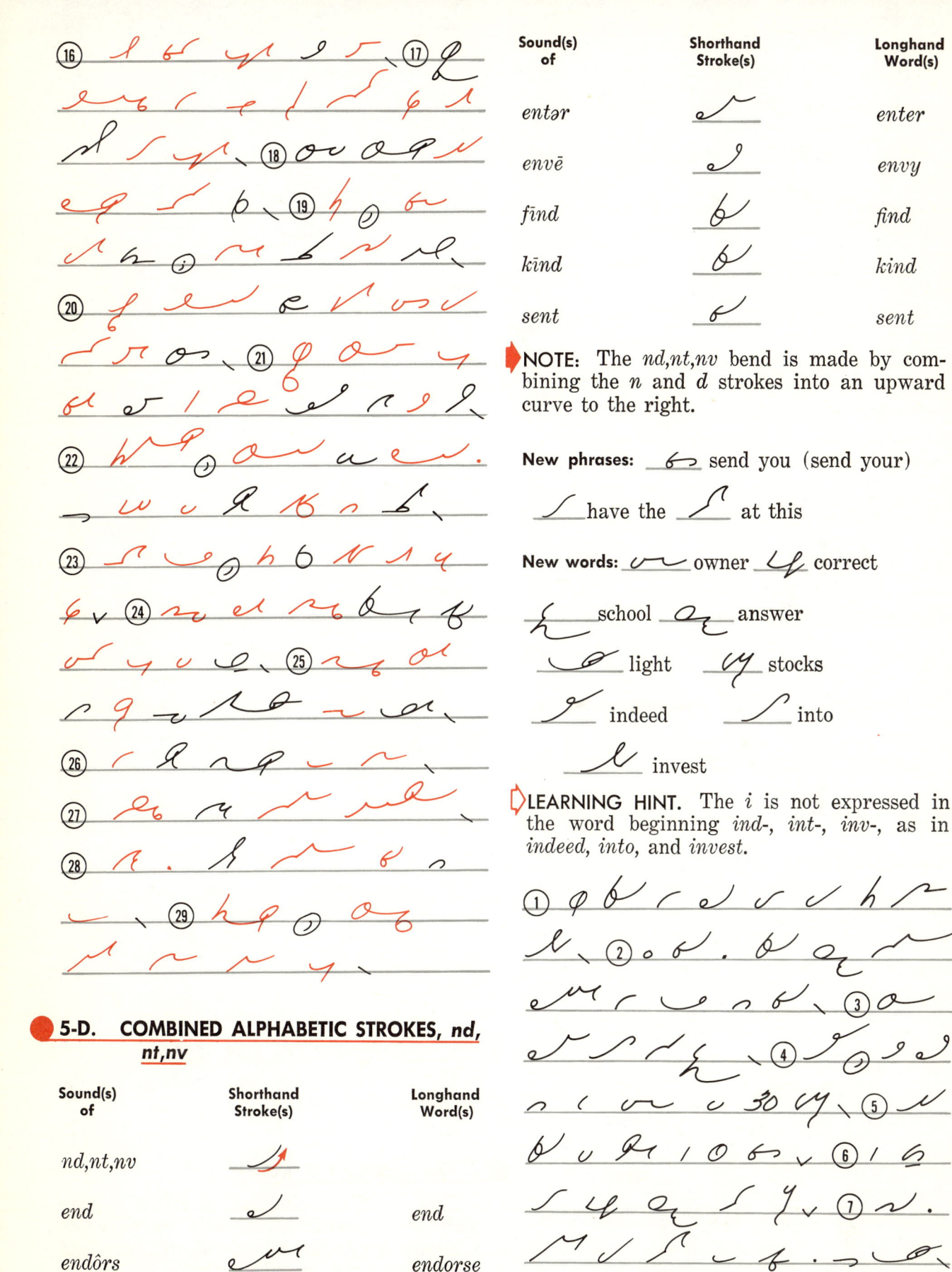

Sound(s) of	Shorthand Stroke(s)	Longhand Word(s)
entər	⌒	enter
envē	⌒	envy
fīnd	⌒	find
kīnd	⌒	kind
sent	⌒	sent

▶ **NOTE:** The *nd, nt, nv* bend is made by combining the *n* and *d* strokes into an upward curve to the right.

New phrases: ⌒ send you (send your)

⌒ have the ⌒ at this

New words: ⌒ owner ⌒ correct

⌒ school ⌒ answer

⌒ light ⌒ stocks

⌒ indeed ⌒ into

⌒ invest

▷ **LEARNING HINT.** The *i* is not expressed in the word beginning *ind-*, *int-*, *inv-*, as in *indeed*, *into*, and *invest*.

5-D. COMBINED ALPHABETIC STROKES, *nd, nt, nv*

Sound(s) of	Shorthand Stroke(s)	Longhand Word(s)
nd, nt, nv	⌒	
end	⌒	end
endôrs	⌒	endorse

LESSON 5   **Page 18**

77-D. PREPARATION FOR LESSON 78

Use the same study procedures as for the two preceding lessons.

77-D-1. SPELLING RULES

Rule 4. If the singular of either a common or a proper noun ends in *s* or an *s* sound (such as *ss*, *x*, *sh*, *ch*, *z*), add *es* to form the plural.

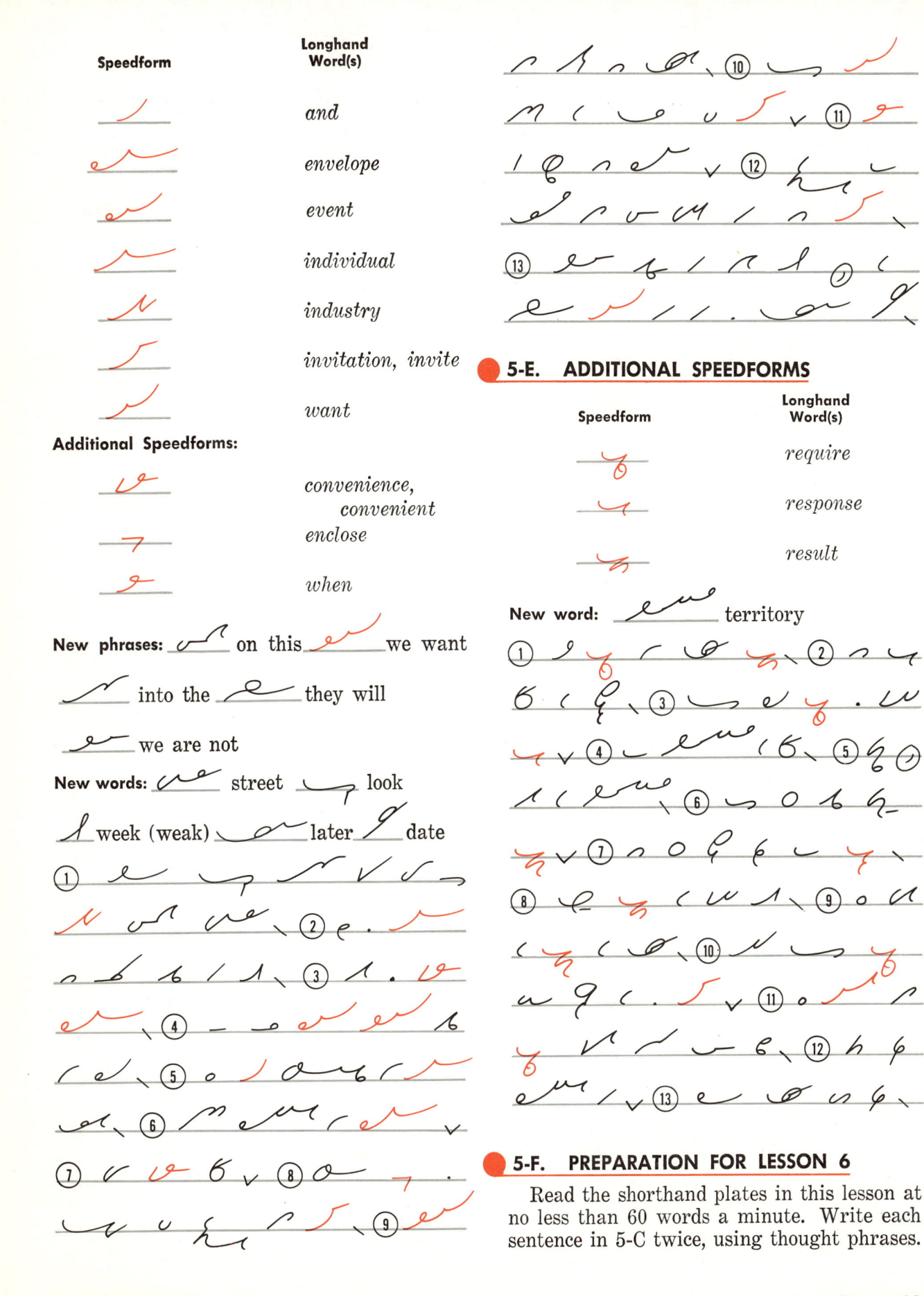

Speedform	Longhand Word(s)
	and
	envelope
	event
	individual
	industry
	invitation, invite
	want

Additional Speedforms:

	convenience, convenient
	enclose
	when

New phrases: on this　　we want　　into the　　they will　　we are not

New words: street　look　week (weak)　later　date

5-E. ADDITIONAL SPEEDFORMS

Speedform	Longhand Word(s)
	require
	response
	result

New word: territory

5-F. PREPARATION FOR LESSON 6

Read the shorthand plates in this lesson at no less than 60 words a minute. Write each sentence in 5-C twice, using thought phrases.

LESSON 5　　　　　　　　　　　　　　　　Page 19

LESSON 77

LESSON 6

6-A. RECAP OF LESSON 5

New phrases: in his, in your (in you), we could, when you (when your)

New words: said, us

The end of a paragraph is indicated by:

6-B. ADDITIONAL SPEEDFORMS

Speedform	Longhand Word(s)
	accord
	advance
	consider
	construct
	correspond, correspondence
	count
	custom
	develop
	difficult
	quantity

New phrases: do you know, of any, with our, with you (with your)

New words: ask, Kay, favor, Dear, accordance

LESSON 6   Page 20

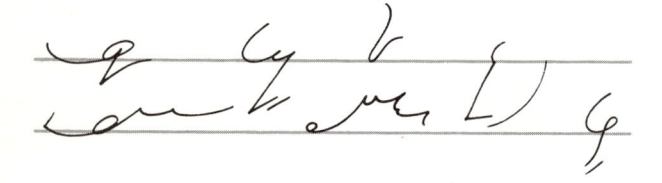

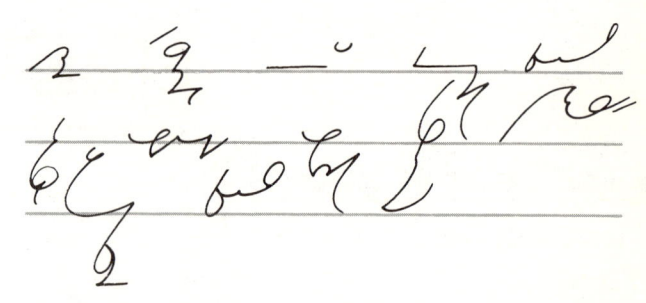

lifetime, projected, growth, signature, collateral, endorsers, preferred, tuition, transactions, moreover, comfortable, currently, specialize, restrict, reputable, background, demonstrated, obligations, faraway

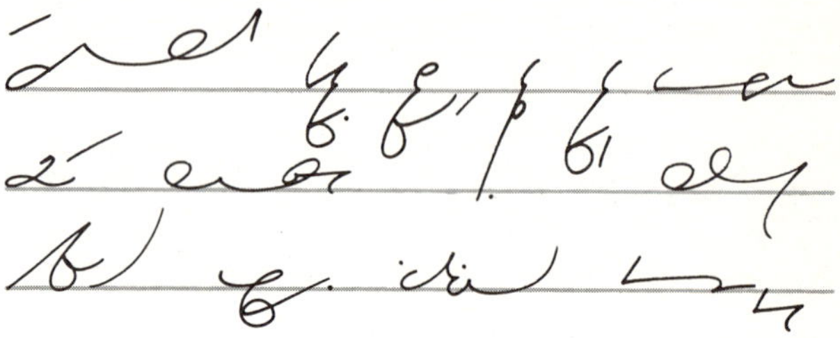

transatlantic, participating, expanded, scheduling (CF), sabbatical, semester, second, airlines, available, departure, residing, household, communications

76-D-4. VOCABULARY PREVIEW OF NEW MATERIAL

LESSON 77

77-A. PHRASE-WRITING MASTERY

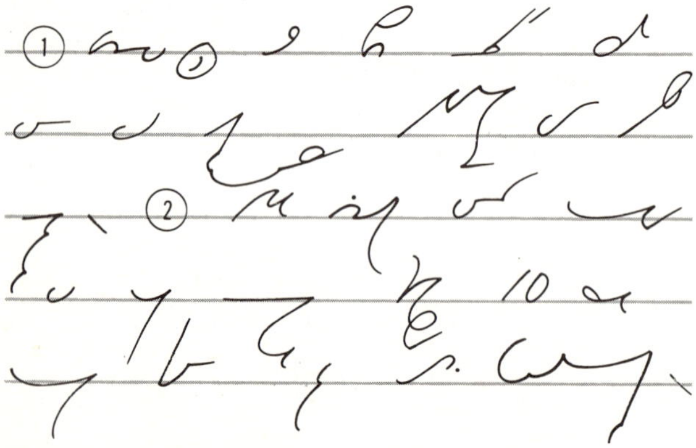

77-B. PREVIEWED NEW DICTATION

Take from dictation material that you previewed in 76-D-4.

77-C. AUTOMATIZATION OF FREQUENTLY USED WORDS

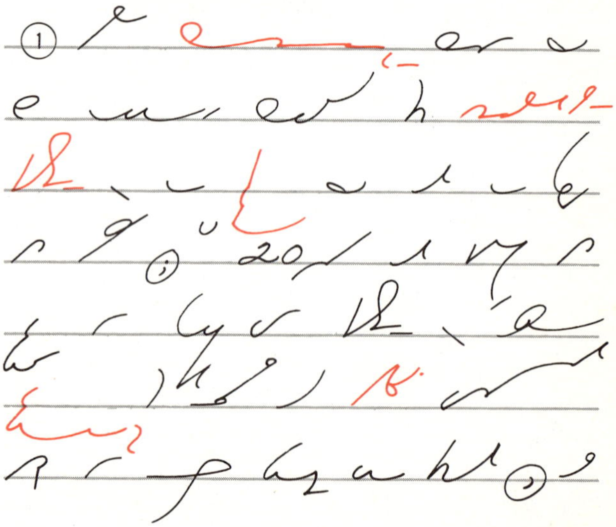

LESSON 77 — Page 227

6-C. THE WORD ENDING -ED

Sound(s) of	Shorthand Stroke(s)	Longhand Word(s)
kərektid		corrected
endid		ended
rātid		rated

NOTE: The sounds of the word ending -ed are expressed by a disjoined upward diagonal.

A hyphen is expressed by:

New phrases: of those   I wanted

New words: air   all   dean   cards   Dallas   techniques   courtesy   trophies   style   cost   though   follow   says   signs   defense   factory   design

LESSON 6 **Page 21**

LESSON 76

6-D. PREPARATION FOR LESSON 7

Be able to read the plates in this lesson at no less than 60 words a minute. Write each phrase and word listed at the beginning of each exercise 3 consecutive times; then write the sentences in 6-C, using the "double thought" phrase procedure.

LESSON 7

7-A. RECAP OF LESSON 6

New phrases: we received — to return — through the

New words: receipt — saw

LESSON 7 — Page 22

76-D-1. SPELLING RULES

Rule 2. If the final *y* in a root word follows a consonant, change the *y* to *i* before all endings except those beginning with *i*. If the final *y* in a root word is preceded by *i*, the *y* is usually retained.

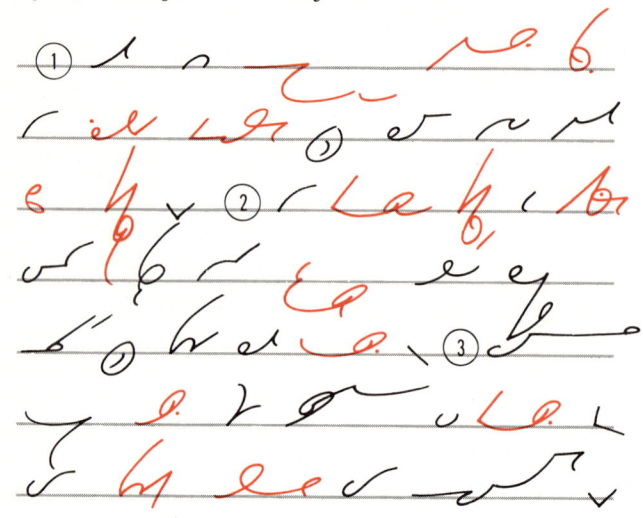

Rule 3. If a word ending begins with a consonant, do not double the final consonant of the root word.

76-D-2. THEORY REVIEW

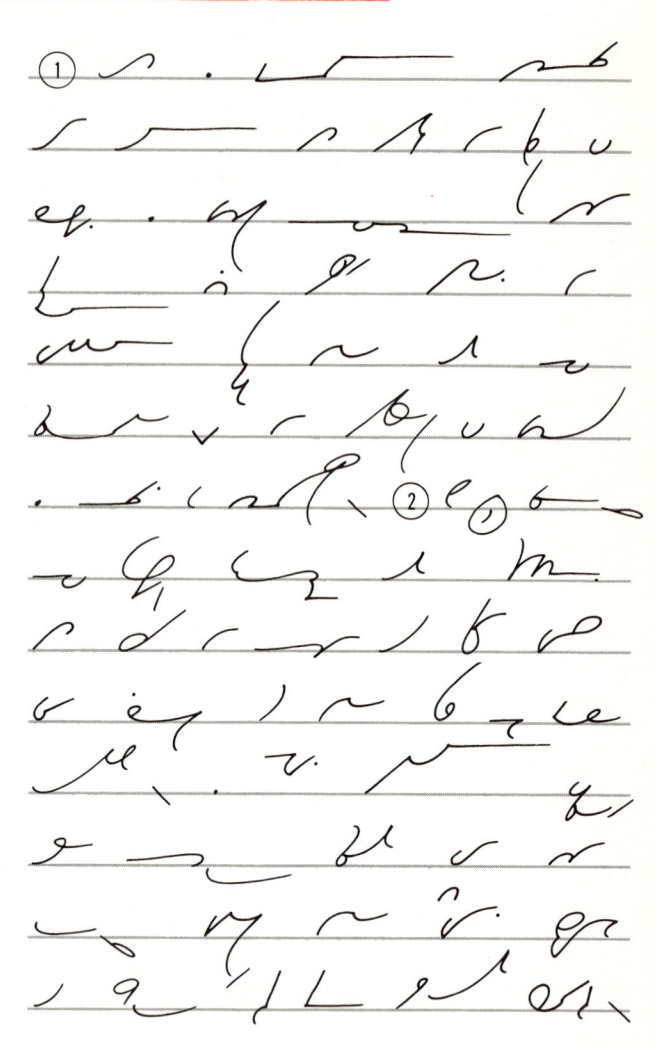

76-D-3. OFFICE-STYLE NOTES

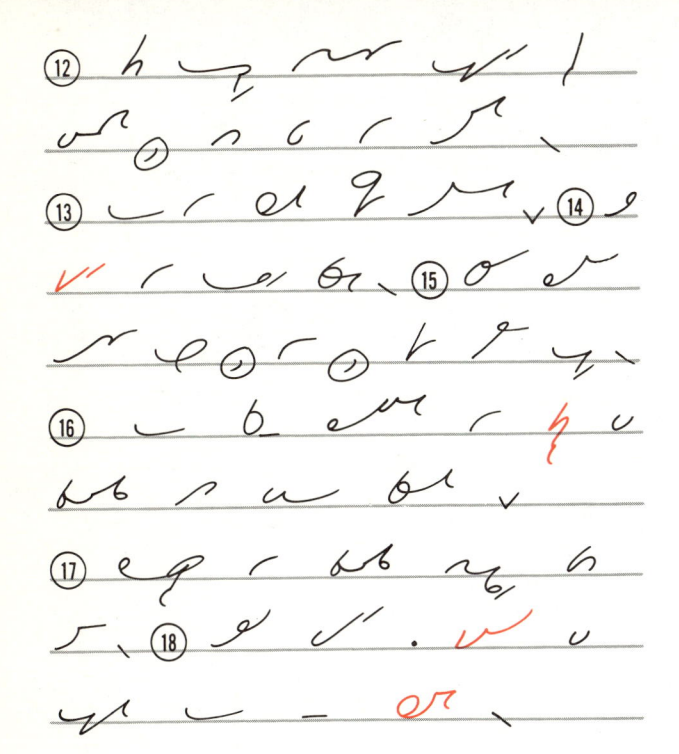

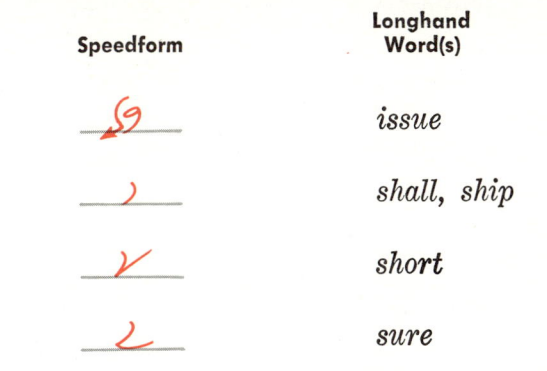

Speedform	Longhand Word(s)
	issue
	shall, ship
	short
	sure

New phrases: as you know — I shall — of this — we shall — I wish — you want — we should like

New words: share — cash — dozen — sheets — clear — tickets — fair (fare) — shown

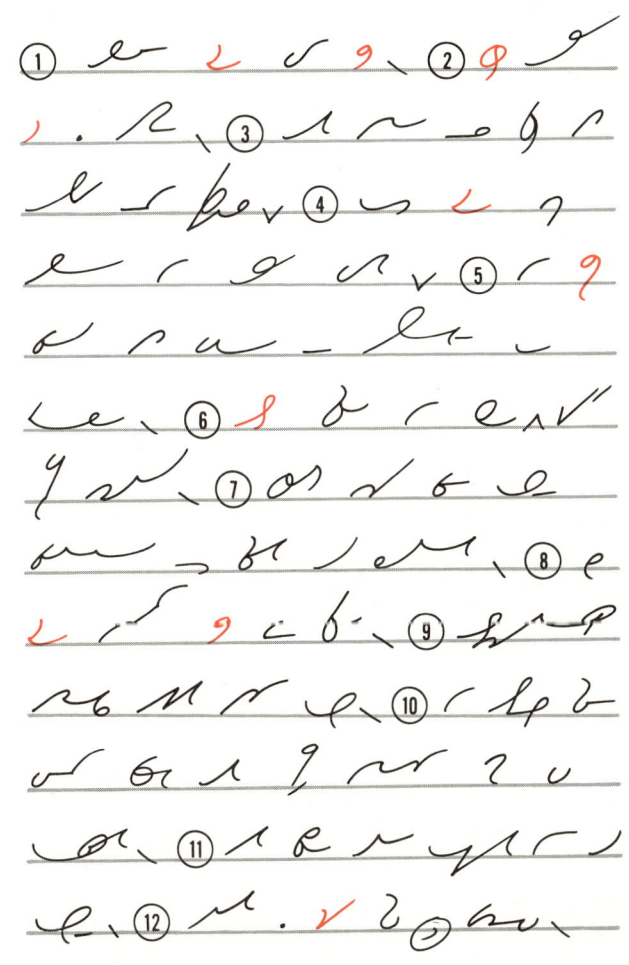

7-B. SHORTHAND ALPHABET

Sound(s) of	Shorthand Stroke(s)	Longhand Word(s)
sh, zh		
lēzhər		leisure
shůd		should
wish		wish

▶ **NOTE:** The sounds of *sh, zh* are expressed by a short downward curve to the right.

New phrases: I should like — when will

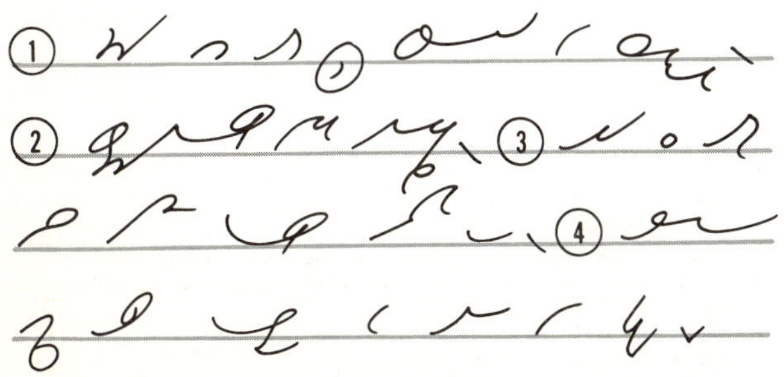

LESSON 7   Page 23

76-D. PREPARATION FOR LESSON 77

Use the same procedures for the following exercises as you have before.

LESSON 76

7-C. THE WORD ENDINGS -SION, -TION

Sound(s) of	Shorthand Stroke(s)	Longhand Word(s)
-shən, -zhən		
ədishən		addition
dəvizhən		division
stāshən		station
teləvizhən		television

▶ **NOTE:** The word endings *-sion, -tion* are expressed by combining the *sh* and *n* strokes.

New phrases: _____ should have _____ he said

New words: _____ start _____ association _____ listen _____ reservation _____ consideration _____ construction _____ visit _____ third _____ additional

7-D. THE WORD ENDING -ING

Sound(s) of	Shorthand Stroke(s)	Longhand Word(s)
fīnding		finding
sēing		seeing
ūzing		using

▶ **NOTE:** The word ending *-ing* is expressed by a dot at the end of the outline.

New phrases: _____ I should have _____ as to the _____ you could

New words: _____ courses _____ since _____ routes _____ latest _____ wrote _____ eat _____ were

LESSON 7 Page 24

LESSON 76

Page 223

7-E. PREPARATION FOR LESSON 8

Be able to read the plates in this lesson at no less than 70 words a minute.

Write each outline in the phrase and word lists 3 consecutive times; then write the sentences in 7-C and 7-D in "double thought" phrases.

LESSON 8

8-A. NOTETAKING CONCENTRATION (LESSONS 1-5)

Write in "double thought" phrases. Do not look in the textbook while you are writing. After writing, check the correctness of your notes.

Use your free hand to manipulate your notebook so that your writing arm is always in the best position for writing.

LESSON 8
Page 25

75-D-4. VOCABULARY PREVIEW OF NEW MATERIAL

convene, equipment, rental, audio-visual, sound, silent, projectors, opaque, circuit, theater, thoroughly, prepaid, brochure, showdate

LESSON 76

76-A. PHRASE-WRITING MASTERY

Automatic phrase writing will speed both note taking and transcription. If you can take each sentence from dictation in 15 seconds, you are recording at the rate of 80 wam; in 12 seconds, at 100 wam, in 10 seconds, at 120 wam.

76-B. PREVIEWED NEW DICTATION

Your teacher will dictate to you new material previewed in 75-D-4.

76-C. AUTOMATIZATION OF FREQUENTLY USED WORDS

The two letters and the memo in the plates contain many of the 1500 most frequently used words in business communication. Try to increase your note recording rate.

LESSON 76 Page 222

8-B. NOTETAKING CONCENTRATION (LESSONS 1-6)

[Shorthand notes, items 1-11]

8-C. NOTETAKING CONCENTRATION (LESSONS 1-7)

[Shorthand notes, items 1-9]

8-D. PREPARATION FOR LESSON 9

Practice reading 8-A, 8-B and 8-C. Instant recognition of an outline must precede your ability to recall that outline when you hear the dictated word.

Write each sentence in 8-B and 8-C in "double thought" phrases. Remember not to look in the textbook as you write; that will cause you to "see" the outline in your mind and remember it later.

Rule 1. *I* before *e*
Except after *c*
Or when sounded like *a*
As in *neighbor* and *weigh*.

> **NOTE:** Some exceptions to the rule are: *either, neither, efficient, foreign, seized, leisure, weird, conscience.*

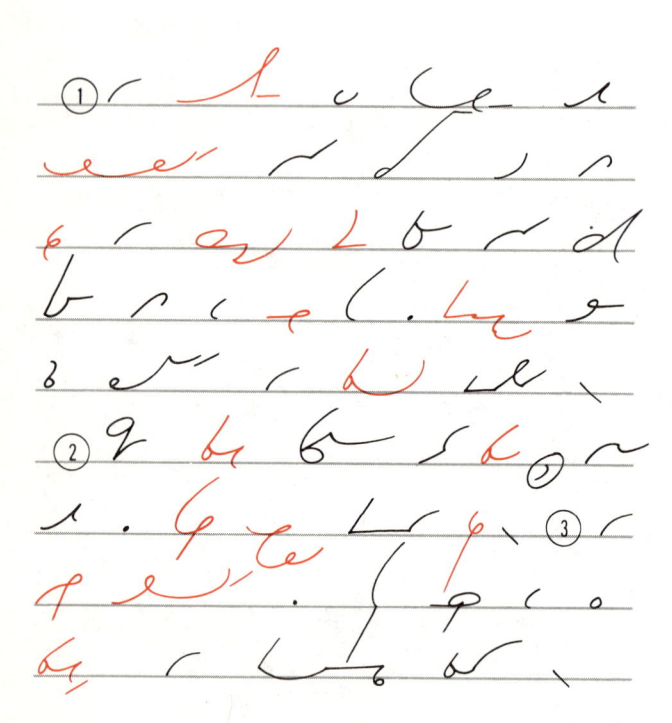

75-D-2. THEORY REVIEW

Transcribe the notes. Then write the notes three times in your notebook.

75-D-3. OFFICE-STYLE NOTES

Read the notes so that you can read them rapidly in class. If the teacher so directs, transcribe the notes into mailable copy.

LESSON 75 Page 221

LESSON 9

9-A. RECAP OF LESSON 7

New phrases: at his, to us, to our, on that

New words: last, lines, selling

9-B. ADDITIONAL SPEEDFORMS

Speedform	Longhand Word(s)
	certificate, certify
	contact
	contract
	control
	convention
	down
	elect
	enough
	found
	next
	notice
	value

New phrases: and have, send us, as you will

New words: dealer, assist, officers, central, leaders

LESSON 9   Page 27

75-D. PREPARATION FOR LESSON 76

The following exercises review some spelling rules and the more difficult theory principles. Also included are problems in office-style notes and a preview of new-matter dictation.

75-D-1. SPELLING RULES

Read the rule presented on the following page, and then transcribe the sentences. The outlines that require application of the rule are in color.

New phrases: I could   I believe

New words: left   war   break (brake)   board   buying   best

9-C. SHORTHAND ALPHABET

Sound(s) of	Shorthand Stroke(s)	Longhand Word(s)
b		
bak		back
bāsis		basis
bilēv		believe
bil		bill

NOTE: The *b* is a large downward stroke, curving to the left. The sound of the word beginning *be-* (bi) is also expressed by the *b* stroke.

Speedform	Longhand Word(s)
	about
	be, been, by
	business

New phrases: I will not be able   to be   I have been   this will be   I will be   there will be   by the   I have been able   with his

New words: read (reed)   rally   difficulty   drive   real   book   bonds   better   but

LESSON 9

Page 28

74-D-6. VOCABULARY PREVIEW OF NEW MATERIAL

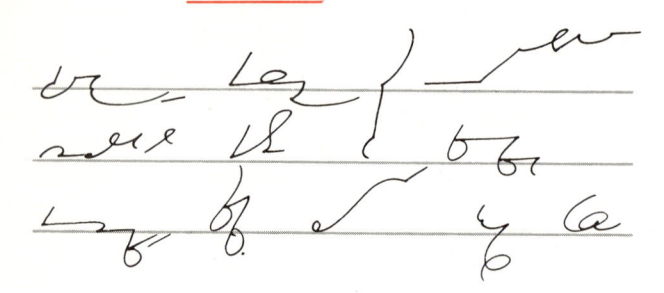

Council, financial, graduates, midwestern, universities, Foundation, campaigns, communicated, gratifying, evident, surpass, prior, gratitude, alumni, spoken, inspiration, faculty, loyalty, tangible, sympathetic, Alma Mater, restricted, scholarships, unrestricted, whatever, citizenry

LESSON 75

75-A. THE 20-WORD SPRINT

75-B. PREVIEWED NEW DICTATION

You will take from dictation the material that you previewed in 74-D-6.

75-C. THE 350-WORD DASH

LESSON 75   Page 219

9-D. PREPARATION FOR LESSON 10

Be able to read the plates in this lesson at no less than 70 words a minute.

Write each outline in the phrase and word lists 3 consecutive times; then write the sentences in 9-A and 9-C in thought phrases.

LESSON 10

10-A. RECAP OF LESSON 9

New phrases: we shall have, of course

New words: decision, assure, Sally, staff

74-D-2. WORD SELECTION

> NOTE: These notes use the words presented in Lesson 70.

74-D-3. SPELLING

> NOTE: The ending -berg (-burg, -burgh) for a proper name is written (; the ending -field is written /.

74-D-4. ABBREVIATIONS

You have already learned some abbreviations. Here are some of those and a few others with which you should be familiar. Write each one 3 times in your notebook.

TV ___ a.m. ___ OK (okay) ___ U.S. ___
f.o.b. ___ p.s. ___ etc. ___ no. ___
p.m. ___ c.c. ___

74-D-5. DERIVATIVE DEVELOPMENT

LESSON 74 — Page 218

Additional Speedform:

⟶ information

New phrases: ___ we have been ___ about the ___ should not be ___ for this ___ for your (for you) ___ we would like

① ② ③

10-B. MODIFIED ALPHABETIC STROKE, fr

Sound(s) of	Shorthand Stroke(s)	Longhand Word(s)
fr, fər, fôr		for
efərts		efforts
frē		free
frāt		freight
frend		friend
ôfər		offer

▶ NOTE: The *fr* bend is made by curving the *f* to the right.

New phrases: ___ they will be ___ have not been ___ that will be ___ by your (by you) ___ do you have

New word: ___ added

① ② ③ ④ ⑤

10-C. SHORTHAND ALPHABET

Sound(s) of	Shorthand Stroke(s)	Longhand Word(s)
m	⟶	
măd		made
māk		make
mā		may
mī		my
sum		some

▶ NOTE: The *m* is a middle-sized straight stroke written forward.

New phrase: ___ to come

New word: ___ businessman

LESSON 10   Page 30

74-D. PREPARATION FOR LESSON 75

These exercises conclude the problems dealing with basic punctuation rules, word differentiation, spelling, and derivative development. In 74-D-4 the writing of some common abbreviations is explained.

74-D-1. PUNCTUATION

▶ NOTE: Rule 25 must be applied.

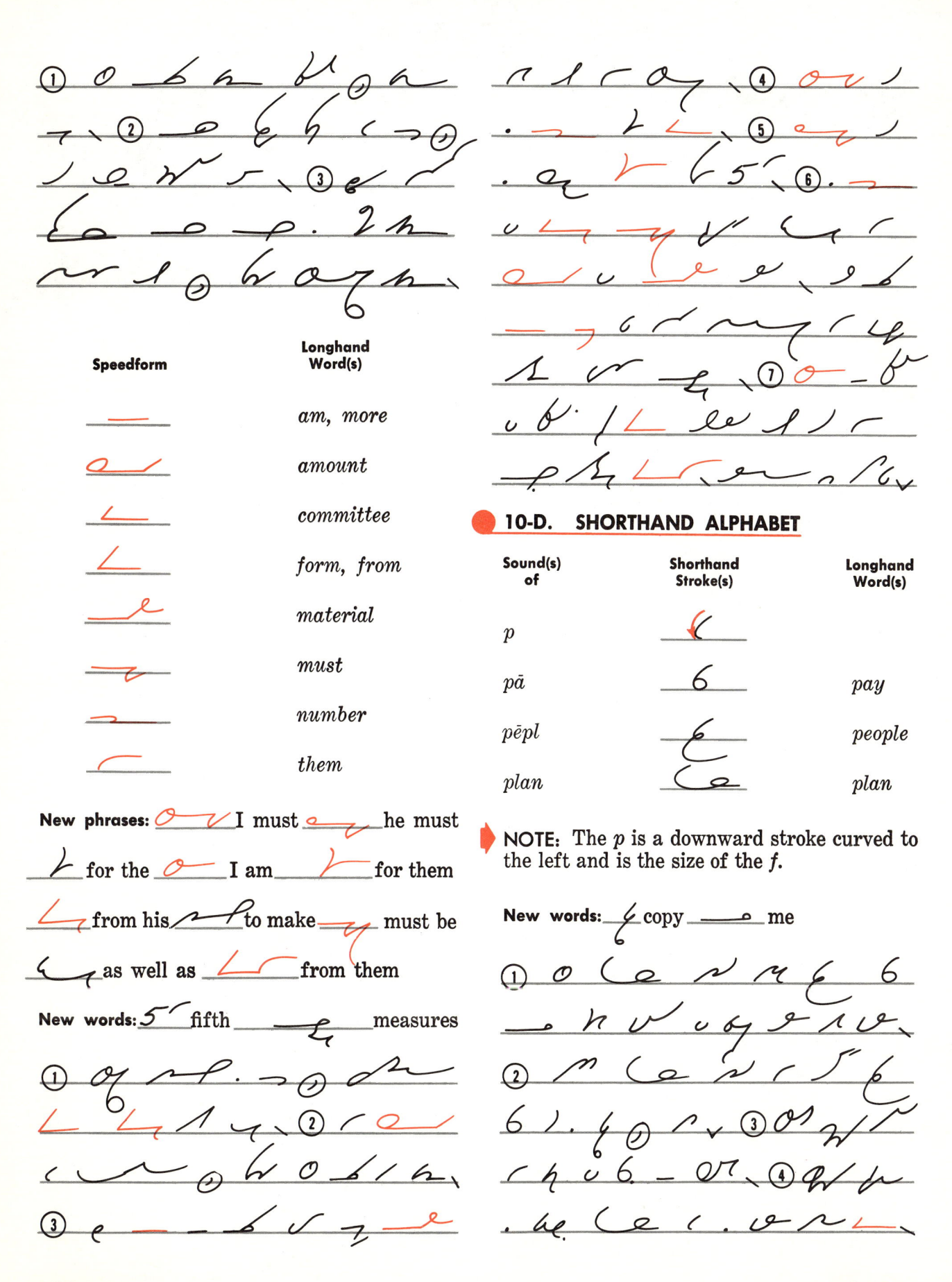

Speedform	Longhand Word(s)
—	am, more
⌒	amount
⌐	committee
∟	form, from
⌒	material
~	must
═	number
⌒	them

New phrases: I must, he must, for the, I am, for them, from his, to make, must be, as well as, from them

New words: 5 fifth, measures

10-D. SHORTHAND ALPHABET

Sound(s) of	Shorthand Stroke(s)	Longhand Word(s)
p	(	
pā	6	pay
pēpl	6	people
plan	6―	plan

NOTE: The *p* is a downward stroke curved to the left and is the size of the *f*.

New words: copy, me

LESSON 10 — Page 31

73-D-5. DERIVATIVE DEVELOPMENT

73-D-6. VOCABULARY PREVIEW OF NEW MATERIAL

Watkins, machines, into the, spring, Simpson, binder, lister, mower, outside, guarantee, justified, genuine, stamped, original, patterns, forgotten, quick, regulation

LESSON 74

74-A. THE 20-WORD SPRINT

74-B. PREVIEWED NEW DICTATION
Your teacher will dictate to you new material previewed in 73-D-6.

74-C. THE 350-WORD DASH

Speedform	Longhand Word(s)
	appreciate
	company
	hope
	please
	public, publish

New phrases: I hope ___ appreciate the ___ appreciate your (appreciate you) ___ to publish ___ I hope you will ___ to please ___ we must ___ to pay ___ and the

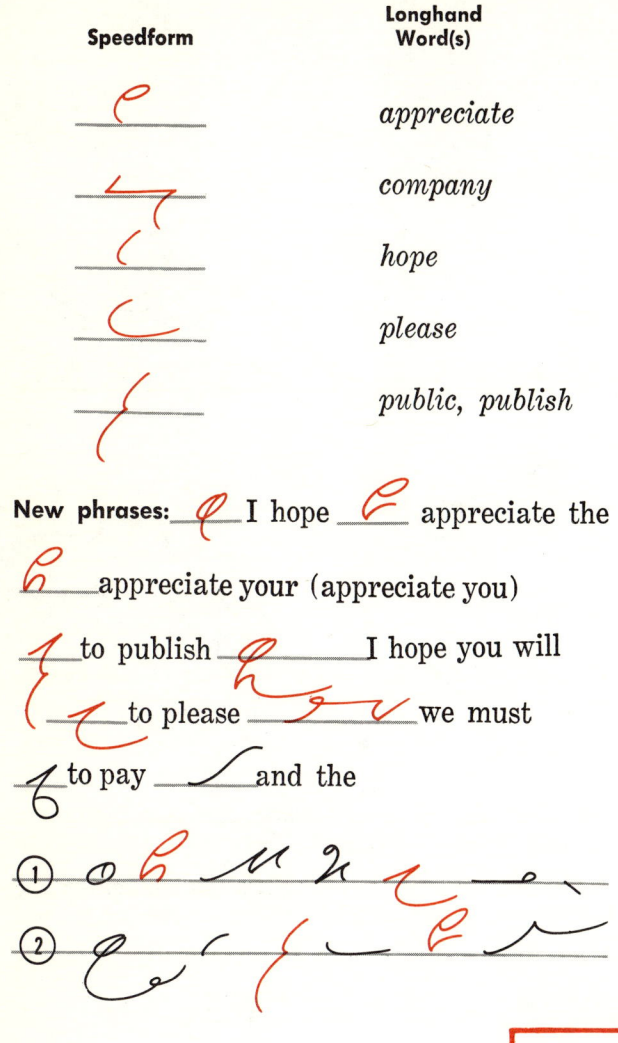

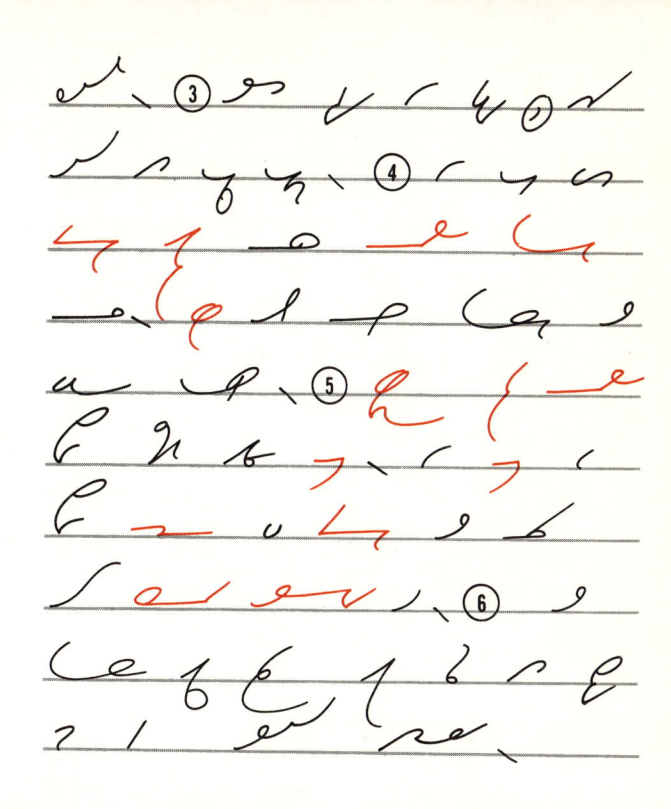

①

②

10-E. PREPARATION FOR LESSON 11

Be able to read the plates in this lesson at no less than 70 words a minute.

Write each preview outline 3 consecutive times; then write the sentences in 10-A, 10-C, and 10-D in "double thought" phrases.

LESSON 11

11-A. RECAP OF LESSON 10

New phrases: ___ by them ___ when the ___ make the ___ will you please ___ of these

New words: ___ solution ___ steps ___ taken ___ print ___ face

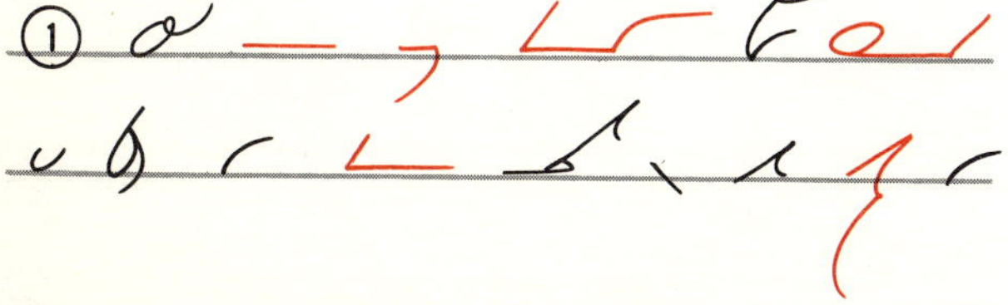

①

②

LESSON 11   Page 32

73-D-2. WORD SELECTION

> NOTE: The notes include application of words shown in Lessons 69 and 70.

73-D-3. SPELLING

> NOTE: In geographical names, *New* is written ———.

73-D-4. PHONETIC STUDIES

desəlit
desəlāt ①

rāning
rāning ②

inklīnd
inklīnd ③

11-B. SHORTHAND ALPHABET

Sound(s) of	Shorthand Stroke(s)	Longhand Word(s)
h	. (dot)	
help		help
hī		high
hüm		whom

▶ NOTE: The *h* is indicated by a dot; place it above and close to the following stroke. If the *h* is sounded first, write it first.

New phrase: it will be

11-C. SHORTHAND ALPHABET

Sound(s) of	Shorthand Stroke(s)	Longhand Word(s)
ch		
chãr		chair
chekt		checked
ēch		each

▶ NOTE: The *ch* is expressed by a long upward stroke curved to the right.

New phrase: can be

New word: placed

Speedform	Longhand Word(s)
	chairman
	change
	merchandise
	which

LESSON 11 Page 33

73-D. PREPARATION FOR LESSON 74

Again, your homework will increase your command of English fundamentals and expand your shorthand vocabulary.

73-D-1. PUNCTUATION

> NOTE: The following notes require application of Rules 24 and 25.

Additional Speedforms:

_1_ department

_e_ has

_l_ part

New phrases: has been / should be / it has been / we cannot / we do not / I hope that

New words: speech / heads / had / him / here, hear (her) / deciding / known

11-D. SHORTHAND ALPHABET

Sound(s) of	Shorthand Stroke(s)	Longhand Word(s)
g, j	/	
ərānj		arrange
big		big
gāv		gave
job		job
manij		manage

NOTE: The g, j is a long straight stroke written downward.

A dash is indicated by: —

LESSON 11 Page 34

72-D-6. VOCABULARY PREVIEW OF NEW MATERIAL

manufactures, typewriter, meters, themselves, Fidelity, linkage, mountings, variety, directly, device, practical, equipment, ratio, keystrokes, productive, attached, reproduction, we can be, assistance, future

LESSON 73

73-A. THE 20-WORD SPRINT

73-B. PREVIEWED NEW DICTATION
Material you previewed in 72-D-6 will be dictated to you.

73-C. THE 350-WORD DASH

LESSON 73   Page 213

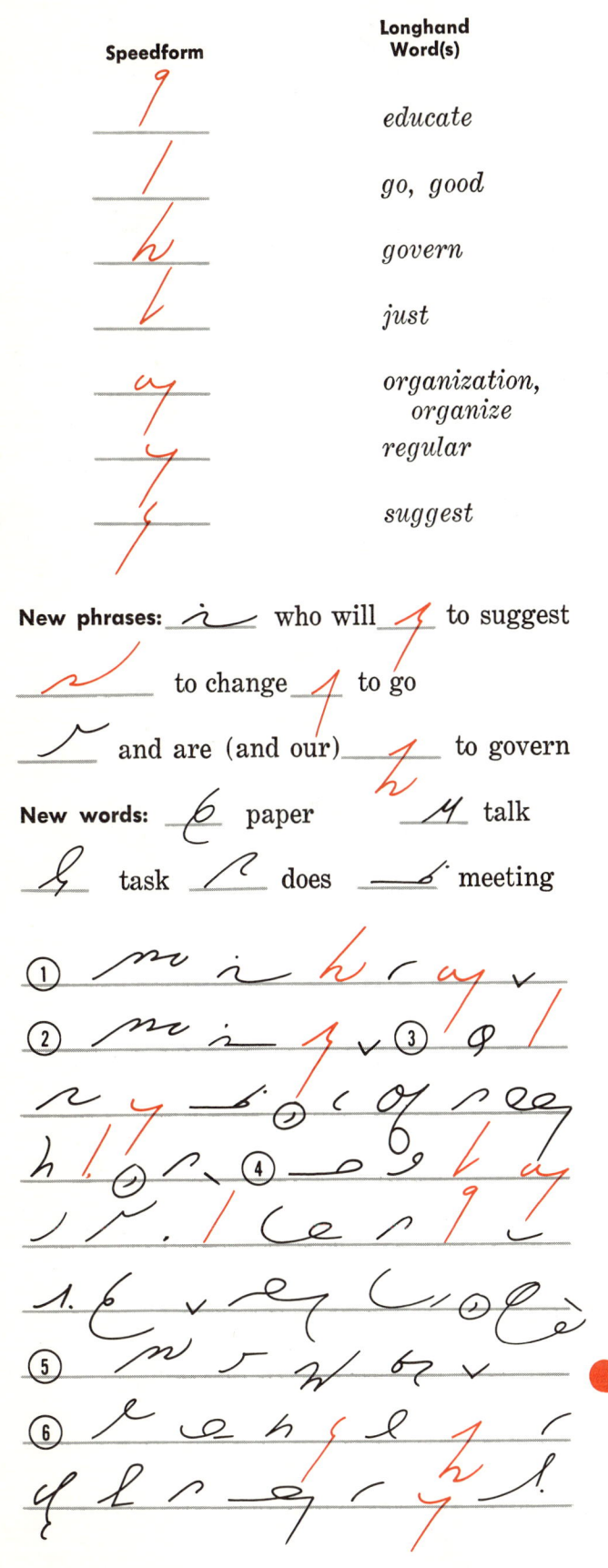

Speedform	Longhand Word(s)
	educate
	go, good
	govern
	just
	organization, organize
	regular
	suggest

New phrases: who will • to suggest • to change • to go • and are (and our) • to govern

New words: paper • talk • task • does • meeting

11-E. PREPARATION FOR LESSON 12

Be able to read the plates in this lesson at no less than 70 words a minute.

Write each preview outline 3 consecutive times; then write 11-C, and 11-D in "double thought" phrases.

LESSON 11 Page 35

72-D-2. WORD SELECTION

> NOTE: The following notes include words presented in Lessons 68-70.

72-D-3. SPELLING

> NOTE: Remember that the ending *-ville* on a proper noun is written _____.

72-D-4. PHONETIC STUDIES

sėrj
sėrj

băd
bad

slā
slā

sō
sō

72-D-5. DERIVATIVE DEVELOPMENT

LESSON 72   Page 212

LESSON 12

● **12-A. NOTETAKING CONCENTRATION**
   (LESSONS 1-9)

Consciously read in thought phrases, thus minimizing the possibility of misreading an outline.

Try to write each individual outline quickly; don't draw it.

[Shorthand outlines numbered 1 through 16]

LESSON 12 — Page 36

72-D. PREPARATION FOR LESSON 73

Again, the exercises strengthen your command of English fundamentals and increase your shorthand vocabulary.

72-D-1. PUNCTUATION

> NOTE: The notes require the application of Rules 23-25.

12-B. NOTETAKING CONCENTRATION (LESSONS 1-10)

12-C. NOTETAKING CONCENTRATION (LESSONS 1-11)

12-D. PREPARATION FOR LESSON 13

Time yourself on reading the notes in 12-A, 12-B, and 12-C. Strive to read steadily as you would if the sentences were in English.

Write each sentence in 12-C in "double thought" phrases. Remember to get a thought phrase in mind and then write the shorthand in your notebook without looking at the notes in the textbook.

71-D-6. VOCABULARY PREVIEW OF NEW MATERIAL

effective, nearest, excluding, holidays, Carpenter, installation, reorganization, procedures, burdened, in the past, popular, volume, dependable, profitable, binders

LESSON 72

72-A. THE 20-WORD SPRINT

72-B. PREVIEWED NEW DICTATION

Your teacher will dictate to you new material previewed in 71-D-6.

72-C. THE 350-WORD DASH

LESSON 72   Page 210

LESSON 13

13-A. RECAP OF LESSON 11

New phrases: he can be / has not been / would be / to get / he will be

New words: set / because / Gentlemen (CF)

▶ **NOTE:** Contracted/correspondence forms (CF) are abbreviated forms provided for certain frequently occurring words such as *Gentlemen*.

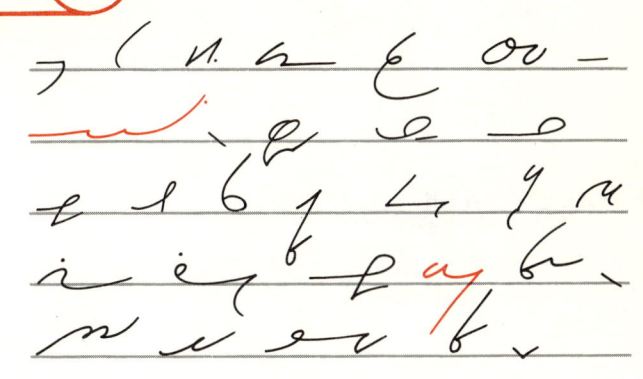

13-B. THE WORD BEGINNING *IN-*

Sound(s) of	Shorthand Stroke(s)	Longhand Word(s)
in-	→	
inkum		income
inkrēsing		increasing

▶ **NOTE:** The *n* stroke is used for the word beginning *in-*.

New word: informed

LESSON 13   Page 38

71-D-2. WORD SELECTION

▶ NOTE: You will need to use the words presented in Lessons 67-70.

71-D-3. SPELLING

▶ NOTE: As you will remember, *port* as a prefix or suffix in a proper name is written ⌒.

71-D-4. PHONETIC STUDIES

əloud
əloud ①

răz
răz ②

dēsnt
disent ③

rōt
rōt ④

bou
bou ⑤

71-D-5. DERIVATIVE DEVELOPMENT

LESSON 71

13-C. THE WORD ENDING -LY

Sound(s) of	Shorthand Stroke(s)	Longhand Word(s)
-lē		
èrlē		early
ēzlē		easily
entīrlē		entirely
famlē		family
ōnlē		only

NOTE: The ending *-ly* is expressed by modifying the *e* circle into a loop, unless the *l* is part of the root word, as in *simply*.

New words: cover, weekly, support, operation, miles, trip, sincerely (CF), definitely

13-D. COMBINED ALPHABETIC STROKES, *mm, mn*

Sound(s) of	Shorthand Stroke(s)	Longhand Word(s)
mm, mn		men
menē, munē		many, money
membərz		members

NOTE: The *mm, mn* blend is a long, straight forward stroke combining *m* and *n*.

New phrase: of them

New words: away, keep, applied, John, meant

LESSON 13

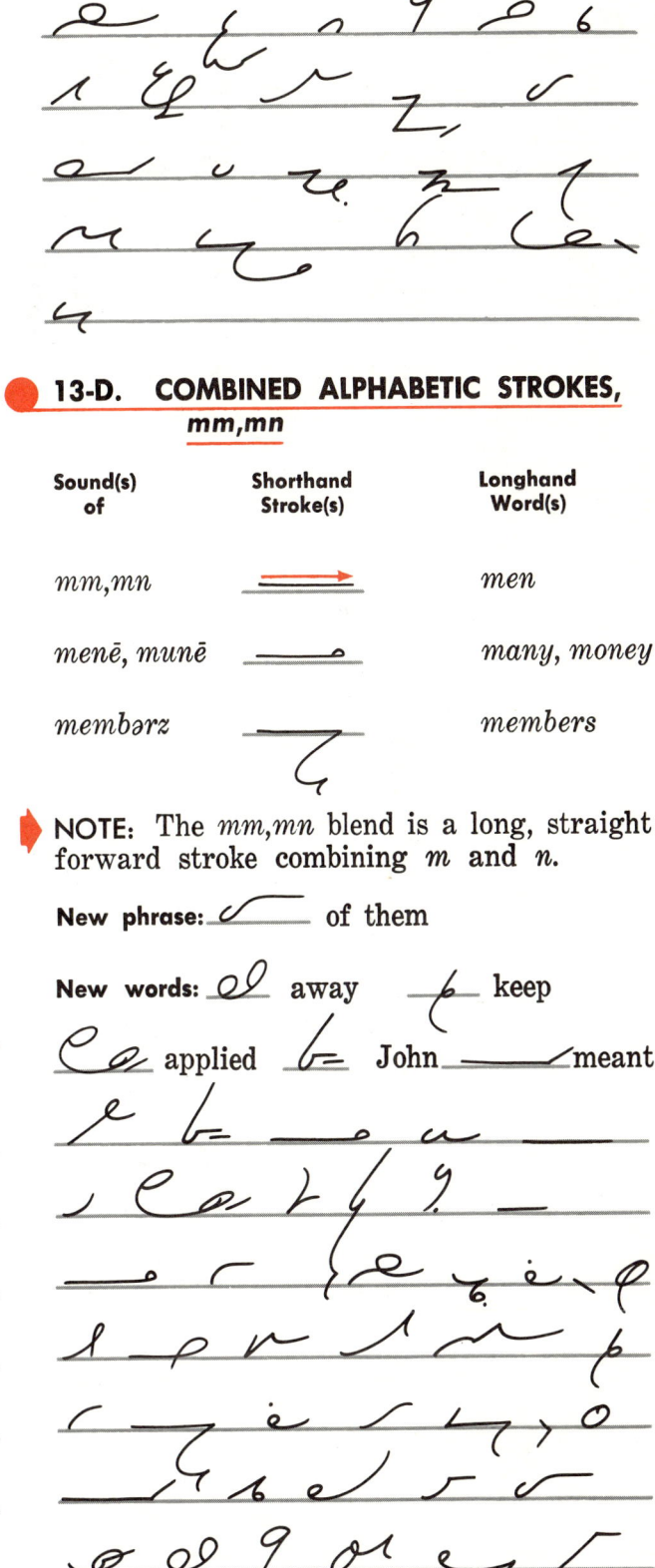

Page 39

71-D. PREPARATION FOR LESSON 72

Continue strengthening your command of English fundamentals and increasing your shorthand vocabulary.

71-D-1. PUNCTUATION

NOTE: The notes require application of Rules 22-25.

Speedform	Longhand Word(s)
╌╌╌	administer
╌╌╌	manufacture

New words: ╌╌╌ month ╌╌╌ chances

╌╌╌ plants

① [shorthand practice lines]

② [shorthand practice lines]

13-E. THE WORD ENDING -MENT

Sound(s) of	Shorthand Stroke(s)	Longhand Word(s)
-mənt	→	
eləmənt	╌╌	element
investmənt	╌╌	investment
manijmənt	╌╌	management

▶ **NOTE:** The ending *-ment* is expressed by the *mn* stroke.

New words: ╌╌╌ requirements

╌╌╌ statement ╌╌╌ government

[shorthand practice lines]

13-F. ADDITIONAL SPEEDFORMS

Speedform	Longhand Word(s)
╌╌╌	contribute
╌╌╌	distribute
╌╌╌	instruct
╌╌╌	mortgage
╌╌╌	special

New phrases: ╌╌╌ we hope ╌╌╌ your letter

New words: ╌╌╌ payments

╌╌╌ instructions

① [shorthand practice lines]

LESSON 13   **Page 40**

70-D-6. VOCABULARY PREVIEW OF NEW MATERIAL

prominent, giftwrap, manufacturer, survey, variety, it would be, if you would, brief, questionnaire, postpaid, postcard, quite, frankly, attempts, knowledge, distribution, one of the, hundreds, variables, market, eventually, retailer, if you have, additional, cooperation, gratefully

LESSON 71

71-A. THE 20-WORD SPRINT

71-B. PREVIEWED NEW DICTATION

Material you previewed in 70-D-6 will be dictated to you.

71-C. THE 350-WORD DASH

13-G. PREPARATION FOR LESSON 14

Expand your reading rate to 80 wam on 13-A; to 70 wam on the other plates. Write each preview outline 3 consecutive times; then write 13-A, 13-C, and 13-F in "double thought" phrases.

LESSON 14

14-A. RECAP OF LESSONS 1-3

New phrases: we know

we will not

14-B. RECAP OF LESSONS 1-7

New word: win

LESSON 14   Page 41

70-D-4. PHONETIC STUDIES

pāshəns
pāshənts ①

əsistəns
əsistənts ②

klōth
klôth ③

pŭl
pül ④

ədishən
idishən ⑤

70-D-3. SPELLING

70-D-5. DERIVATIVE DEVELOPMENT

LESSON 70
Page 206

14-C. RECAP OF LESSONS 1-13

New phrases: to give · to them · has your · from our

New words: Sam · branch · ahead · election · patrons

Please give us your evaluation; we are much in need of your objective assessment.

▶ **NOTE:** The following material also requires application of Rules 21-24.

▶ **70-D-2. WORD SELECTION**

cents—hundredth parts of a dollar
sense—the meaning of the spoken or written word; to understand

▶ **NOTE:** Words shown in Lessons 66-69 will need to be used.

▶ **70-D. PREPARATION FOR LESSON 71**

Once again your homework is designed to help you master English fundamentals and increase your shorthand vocabulary.

▶ **70-D-1. PUNCTUATION**

Rule 25. A semicolon is used between clauses of a compound sentence that are not joined by a conjunction.

LESSON 70

Page 205

New phrase: you will find

● **14-E. ADDITIONAL SPEEDFORMS**

Speedform	Longhand Word(s)
	advantage
	equip
	establish
	immediate, immediately
	importance, important
	opportunity
	report
	situate, situation
	thank, think

New phrase: I think (I thank)

New words: equipment   such   much   fall   first

● **14-D. THE COMPOUND ELEMENT *UNDER***

Sound(s) of	Shorthand Stroke(s)	Longhand Word(s)
undər	(disjoined)	under
undərnēth		underneath
undərtāking		undertaking
undərrīt		underwrite

▶ **NOTE:** The compound element *under* is indicated by a disjoined *u* stroke above the line.

LESSON 14   Page 43

LESSON 70

70-A. THE 20-WORD SPRINT

70-B. PREVIEWED NEW DICTATION

Your teacher will dictate to you new material previewed in 69-D-6.

70-C. THE 350-WORD DASH

14-F. PREPARATION FOR LESSON 15

Be able to read 14-A and 14-B at 80 wam; the other plates at 70 wam.

Write each preview outline 3 consecutive times; then write 14-A and 14-B in "double thought" phrases.

LESSON 15

15-A. RECAP OF LESSON 14

New phrases: to me · you think · to thank you for

(Note omission of dot when *thank* is phrased.)

New words: action · prices · pleasure · adjustment · administration · hand

LESSON 15   Page 44

69-D-3. SPELLING

69-D-4. PHONETIC STUDIES

īdl
īdl ①

rütz
rütz ②

breth
brēth ③

sēm
sēm ④

dizèrt
dezərt ⑤

69-D-5. DERIVATIVE DEVELOPMENT

69-D-6. VOCABULARY PREVIEW OF NEW MATERIAL

fruit, season, superb, century, recipe, bottom, highest, more than, juicy, pineapple, cherries, plump, raisins, pecans, invited, quantity, Christmas, token, avoid, pressure

LESSON 69   Page 203

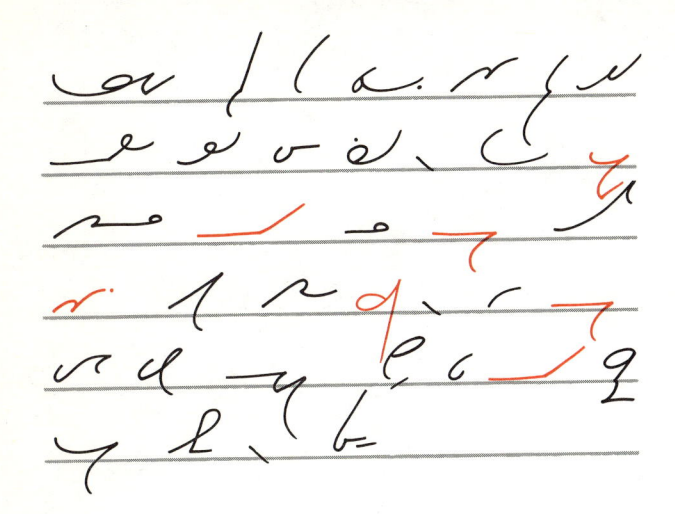

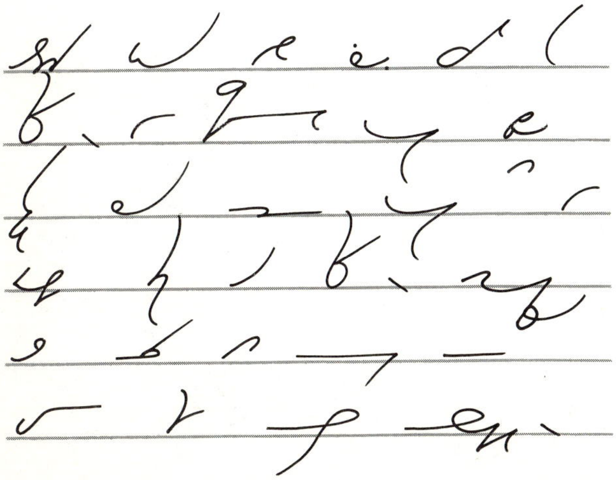

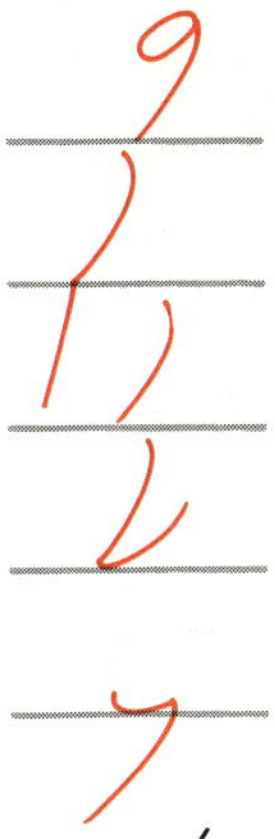

Speedform	Longhand Word(s)
	agriculture
	graduate
	great
	ground
	regard

New phrases: ___ from the ___ for our ___ to select

New words: ___ regret ___ recent ___ agrees ___ up ___ managers

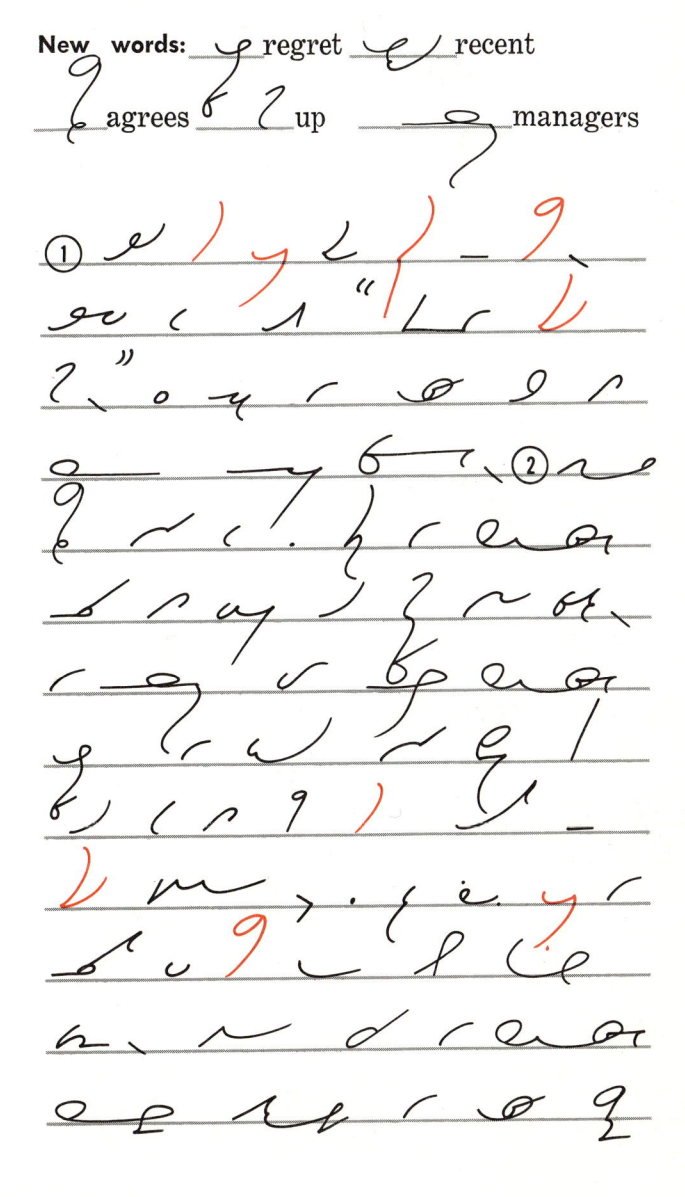

15-B. MODIFIED ALPHABETIC STROKE, gr, jr

Sound(s) of	Shorthand Stroke(s)	Longhand Word(s)
gr, jər		
grād		grade
grüp		group
mā jər		major

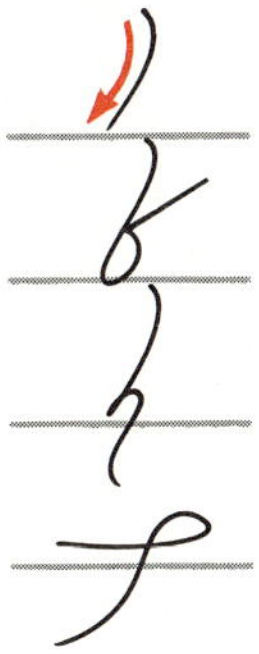

NOTE: The *gr, jr* bend is made by curving the *g, j* stroke to the right.

New words: ___ markets ___ aids

LESSON 15

Page 45

69-D. PREPARATION FOR LESSON 70

Continue the same pattern of study as in the last lesson.

69-D-1. PUNCTUATION

Rule 24. Use a comma to indicate the omission of words necessary for the completeness of a sentence.

The boys sent footballs; the girls, ice skates.

▶ NOTE: The following notes also include applications of Rules 20-23.

69-D-2. WORD SELECTION

passed—moved; gone beyond; transferred from one to another
past—pertaining to a former time; former

▶ NOTE: The notes include words shown in Lessons 65-68 as well as these.

	Speedform	Longhand Word(s)
		anxious

New phrase: ___ to that

New words: ___ session ___ along

15-C. SHORTHAND ALPHABET

Sound(s) of	Shorthand Stroke(s)	Longhand Word(s)
ng		
bring		bring
lông		long
spring		spring

▶ **NOTE:** The *ng* is indicated by a short, straight, downward slanting stroke.

New phrase: ___ one of the

15-D. SHORTHAND ALPHABET

Sound(s) of	Shorthand Stroke(s)	Longhand Word(s)
ngk		
bangk		bank
blangks		blanks
lengkth		length

▶ **NOTE:** The *nk* blend is indicated by a long, straight, downward slanting stroke.

15-E. ADDITIONAL SPEEDFORMS

Speedform	Longhand Word(s)
	approximate
	distinct, distinguish
	employ
	hospital
	improve
	inspect, newspaper
	particular
	respect
	specific, specify

New phrases: ___ who will be ___ more than ___ to improve

New words: ___ means ___ eager ___ habits ___ stories ___ among ___ floor

LESSON 15   **Page 46**

LESSON 69

69-A. THE 20-WORD SPRINT

69-B. PREVIEWED NEW DICTATION

Material you previewed in 68-D-6 will be dictated to you.

69-C. THE 350-WORD DASH

15-F. PREPARATION FOR LESSON 16

Be able to read 15-A and 15-B at 80 wam; the other plates at 70 wam.

Write each preview outline 3 consecutive times; then write 15-A, 15-C, 15-D, and 15-E in "double thought" phrases.

LESSON 16

16-A. NOTETAKING CONCENTRATION (LESSONS 1-13)

Practice reading the notes until you can read fluently.

16-B. NOTETAKING CONCENTRATION (LESSONS 1-14)

LESSON 16 — Page 47

within a state

68-D-3. SPELLING

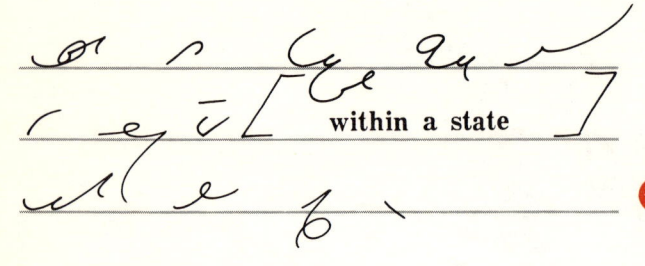

68-D-4. PHONETIC STUDIES

mēn
mēn ①

sālz
sālz ②

pēr
pēr ③

led
led ④

wăv
wăv ⑤

68-D-5. DERIVATIVE DEVELOPMENT

68-D-6. VOCABULARY PREVIEW OF NEW MATERIAL

recently, salesmen, campus, reiterated, solicitors, institutions, jurisdiction, executive, authority, union, library, dormitories, administrative, accordance, wishes, unless, permission, Williams

LESSON 68 **Page 200**

16-C. NOTETAKING CONCENTRATION
(LESSONS 1-15)

16-D. PREPARATION FOR LESSON 17

Be sure you can read fluently all the plate notes in Lesson 16.

Write in "double thought" phrases the notes in 16-B and 16-C.

68-D. PREPARATION FOR LESSON 69

Follow the same procedure that you used in the last lesson.

68-D-1. PUNCTUATION

Rule 23. Use a colon after an introductory expression to indicate that a listing or explanation follows.

I need the following: pens, notebooks, and erasers.

NOTE: You will need to apply Rules 19-22 as well as the one above.

68-D-2. WORD SELECTION

moral—pertaining to *character* or *conduct*
morale—*spirit* or *feeling* of a *person* or *persons*

NOTE: Words shown in Lessons 64-67 will also need to be used.

LESSON 17

17-A. RECAP OF LESSON 15

New phrase: who have been

New words: suggestion, discussion, honor, releases, given

17-B. COMBINED ALPHABETIC STROKES, *tm, tn*

Sound(s) of	Shorthand Stroke(s)	Longhand Word(s)
təm, tən, tn		
əsistənt		assistant
bůlətn		bulletin
ītəm		item
ritn		written

NOTE: The *tm, tn* bend is made by combining the *t* and *m* strokes in a middle-sized upward curve to the left.

Speedform	Longhand Word(s)
	attention
	contain
	stand
	time

New words: standards, lost, supplies, contribution, calls

Page 49

LESSON 68

68-A. THE 20-WORD SPRINT

68-B. PREVIEWED NEW DICTATION

Your teacher will dictate to you new material previewed in 67-D-6.

68-C. THE 350-WORD DASH

17-C. COMBINED ALPHABETIC STROKES, ou, ow

Sound(s) of	Shorthand Stroke(s)	Longhand Word(s)
ou		
əround		around
houzing		housing
pouər		power

▶ **NOTE:** The *ou, ow* stroke is expressed by combining the *o* and *w* strokes.

New words: noon   development

	Speedform	Longhand Word(s)
		announce
		how, out
		throughout

New phrase: to those

17-D. THE WORD BEGINNING EX-

Sound(s) of	Shorthand Stroke(s)	Longhand Word(s)
egz-, eks-		
egzamənāshən		examination
egzampl		example
ekslənt		excellent
eksept		except
eksplān		explain

▶ **NOTE:** The beginning *ex-* is expressed by joining the *e* and *s* strokes.

New phrases: to gain   do you think   who think

LESSON 17   Page 50

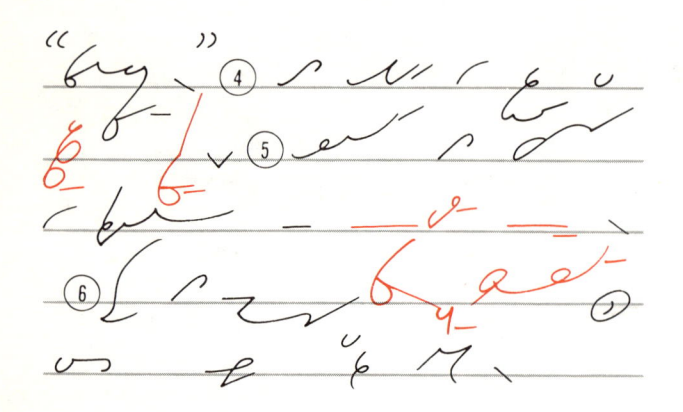

67-D-4. PHONETIC STUDIES

düpləkāt
düplək it

mīnūt
minit

lūs
lūz

bās
bās

sōər
sōər

tēmd
tēmd

67-D-5. DERIVATIVE DEVELOPMENT

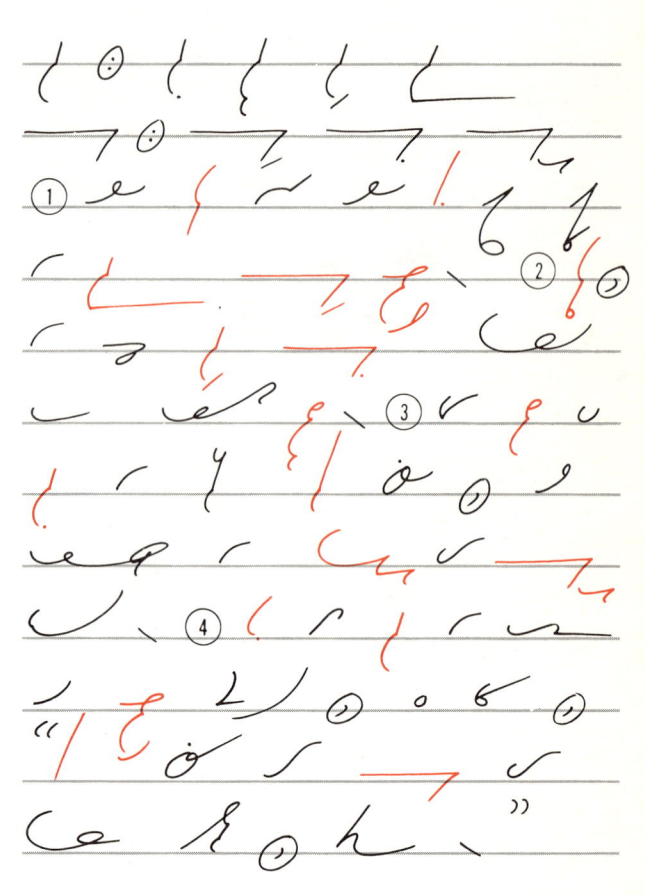

67-D-6. VOCABULARY PREVIEW OF NEW MATERIAL

Advisory, recommended, Directors, appointed, factors, future, development, Lemon, erected, sanitary, marinas, recreational, highest, recommendations, various, shoreline, qualified, assignment, Executive, Chamber, Commerce

LESSON 67

New words: referred   affairs   differences

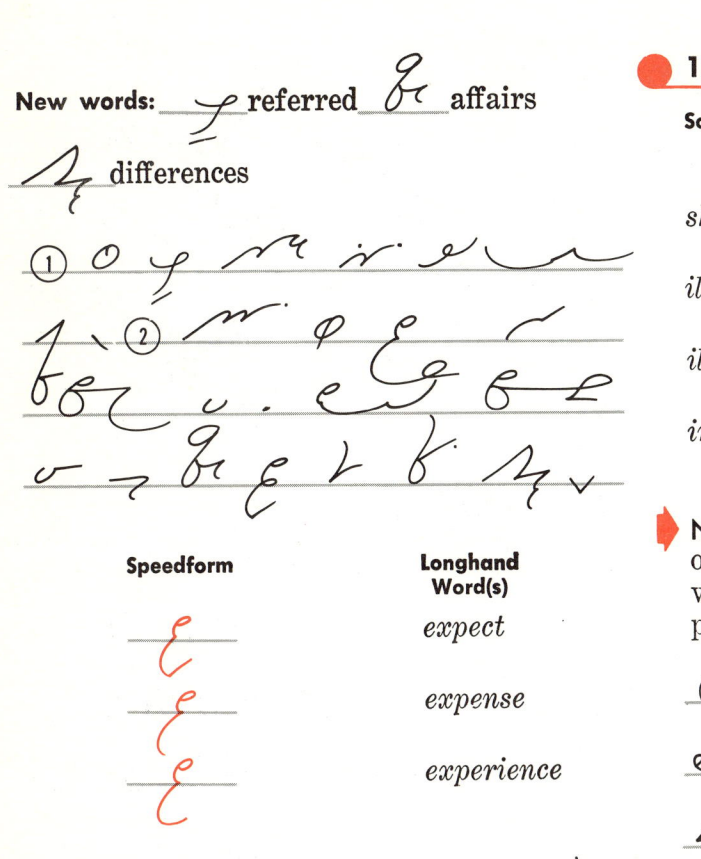

Speedform — **Longhand Word(s)**
expect
expense
experience

17-E. SHORTHAND ALPHABET

Sound(s) of	Shorthand Stroke(s)	Longhand Word(s)
short *i*	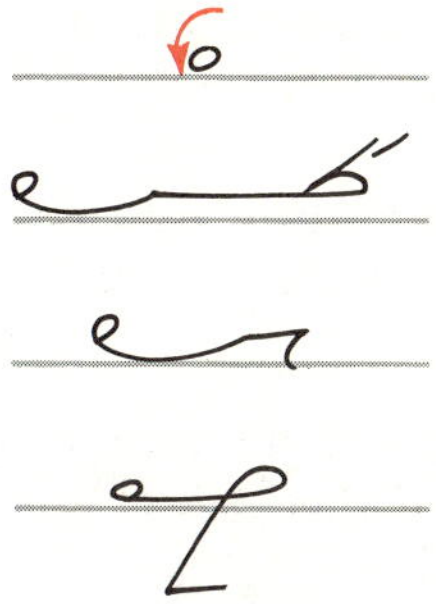	
ilimənātid		eliminated
ilnis		illness
imajən		imagine

NOTE: When the sound of initial longhand *e* or *i* is phonetic short *i*, the small circle is written, except where a word beginning takes precedence such as *into* presented in 5-D.

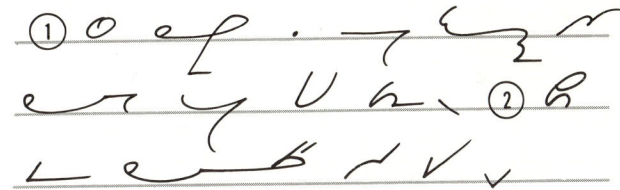

17-F. PREPARATION FOR LESSON 18

Be able to read 17-A at 80 wam; the other plates at 70 wam. Write each preview outline 3 consecutive times; then write 17-C, 17-D, and 17-E in "double thought" phrases.

LESSON 18

18-A. RECAP OF LESSON 17

New words: nation   knowledge   travel   now

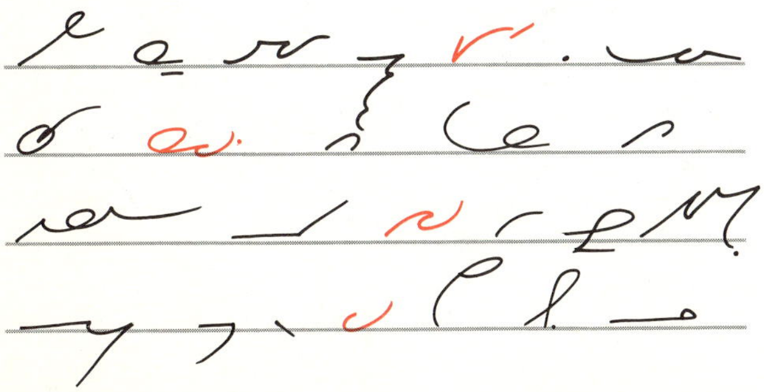

LESSON 18 — Page 51

67-D-1. PUNCTUATION

Rule 22. Use quotation marks to enclose each direct quotation.

He said, "The damage was extensive."
"Can you go," he asked, "if we wait for you?"

NOTE: In the following paragraphs you will need to apply Rules 18-21 as well as the one presented above.

67-D-2. WORD SELECTION

core—the main or center part
corps—a body of individuals, especially a military group

NOTE: The following notes include words shown in Lessons 63-66 as well as those presented above.

67-D-3. SPELLING

LESSON 67

18-B. THE WORD BEGINNINGS PER-, PUR-

Sound(s) of	Shorthand Stroke(s)	Longhand Word(s)
pər-, pėr-		
pərmiting		permitting
pėrsn		person
pėrpəs		purpose

NOTE: The beginnings *per-*, *pur-* are a combination of the *p* and *r* strokes.

New phrases: on his   we wish

New words: college   career

Speedform	Longhand Word(s)
	present
	probable, problem
	product
	prompt
	provide

Additional Speedforms:

active, activity

figure

New phrases: who are   to provide
who would be   to present

New words: buyers   education
seem (seam)   names   appeal
prepare   prefer   precede
profession   proceeds

LEARNING HINT. The word beginning *pre-*, having the sounds of *prē-*, *pri-*, is written   . The word beginning *pro-*, having the sounds of *prō-*, *prə-*, is written   . *Prepare, prefer, precede, profession,* and *proceeds* are examples.

LESSON 18   Page 52

67-D. PREPARATION FOR LESSON 68

Follow the same directions as for the similar exercises in previous lessons.

18-C. COMBINED ALPHABETIC STROKES, dd, dt, td

Sound(s) of	Shorthand Stroke(s)	Longhand Word(s)
ded, det, did, dit, təd	∕	dead, debt, did
ditālz		details
tədā		today

NOTE: The dd, dt, td blend is made by combining the d and t strokes into a slanting straight stroke written upward.

New phrases: to know   for us
New words: study   mistakes

18-D. THE WORD BEGINNINGS INTER-, INTR-

Sound(s) of	Shorthand Stroke(s)	Longhand Word(s)
intər-, intrə-	— (disjoined)	
intərfēr		interfere
intərnashənl		international
intrədukshən		introduction

NOTE: The beginnings *inter-* and *intr-* are expressed by a disjoined *n* stroke above the line.

New phrase: I would not
New word: agreement

Speedform	Longhand Word(s)
	interest

Additional Speedforms:

| | economic, economy |
| | thing |

YOU HAVE NOW LEARNED ALL THE SPEEDFORMS!

LESSON 18   **Page 53**

pérfikt
pərfekt ③

ôltərnāt
ôltərnit ④

əprōprēāt
əprōprēit ⑤

66-D-5. DERIVATIVE DEVELOPMENT

66-D-6. VOCABULARY PREVIEW OF NEW MATERIAL

faculty, students, national, holiday, transportation, especially, dormitory, resident, celebrate, patriotic, substitution, accordance, regularly, charged, campus, announced

LESSON 67

67-A. THE 20-WORD SPRINT

67-B. PREVIEWED NEW DICTATION

Your teacher will dictate to you new material containing the vocabulary words which you previewed in 66-D-6.

67-C. THE 350-WORD DASH

New phrases: of all · in it · from your (from you) · to put

New words: announcement · nothing · introduce · play · anything · booklet · firms · everything · personal · something · minutes

18-E. PREPARATION FOR LESSON 19

Be able to read 18-A and 18-B at 80 wam; the other plates at 70 wam. Write each preview outline 3 consecutive times; then write 18-A, 18-B, 18-C, and 18-D in thought phrases.

LESSON 19

19-A. RECAP OF LESSON 18

New phrase: did not

New words: procedures · data · cut · employment · personnel · credit · period · improvement · mentioned

LESSON 19 — Page 54

66-D-2. WORD SELECTION

all ready—everything or everybody is prepared
already—prior to some specified time

> **NOTE:** The following notes also include the words presented in Lessons 62-65.

[between states]
[within a state]

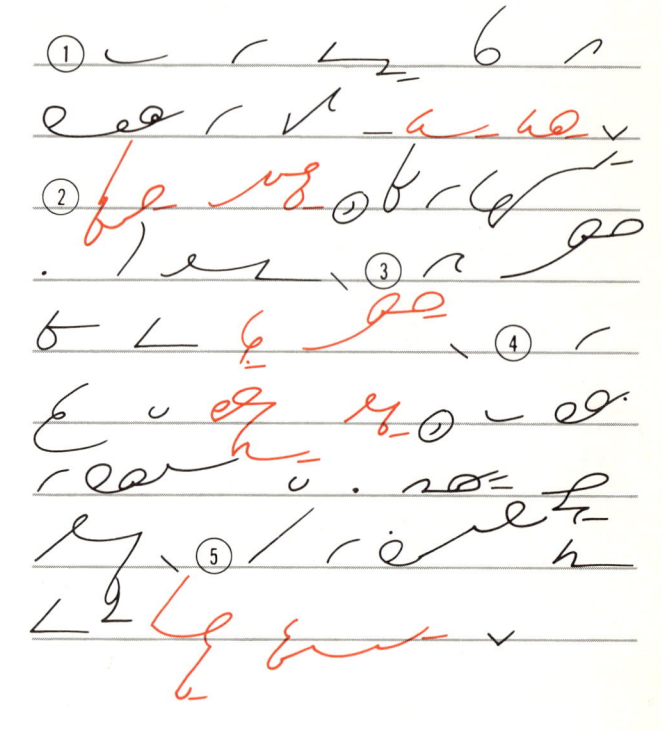

66-D-3. SPELLING

66-D-4. PHONETIC STUDIES

Beginning here, the phonetic studies may involve the same word pronounced either alike or differently according to the part of speech being used.

səspekt
suspekt

sepərāt
sepərit

LESSON 66 — Page 193

19-C. COMBINED ALPHABETIC STROKES, oi, oy

Sound(s) of	Shorthand Stroke(s)	Longhand Word(s)
oi		
boiz		boys
join		join
oil		oil

▶ NOTE: The sounds of *oi, oy* are expressed by combining the *o* and *e* strokes.

New words: crew drilling

19-B. THE WORD BEGINNING UN-

Sound(s) of	Shorthand Stroke(s)	Longhand Word(s)
un-, ən-		
ənles		unless
əntil		until
unūzd		unused

▶ NOTE: The beginning *un-* is expressed by combining the *u* and *n* strokes.

New phrases: may be for those

New words: especially during press revealed box

19-D. THE WORD ENDINGS -THER, -THOR

Sound(s) of	Shorthand Stroke(s)	Longhand Word(s)
-thər		
ənuthər		another
ôthər		author
ēthər		either
fäthər		father
uthər		other

▶ NOTE: The sounds of *-ther, -thor* are expressed by the *th* stroke.

LESSON 19 Page 55

66-D. PREPARATION FOR LESSON 67

Continue the same pattern of study that you followed in Lesson 65.

66-D-1. PUNCTUATION

Rule 21. Use a dash to indicate a sudden change in the structure of a sentence.

A few people—the mayor, the county clerk, and the city manager—favored the action.

▸ NOTE: The following material also requires the application of Rules 17-20.

New phrases: _for that_   _to join_

New words: _open_   _understood_   _space_   _arrangements_   _balance_   _room_   _understand_   _lack_

19-E   FREQUENT ABBREVIATIONS

Following a number or a symbol, *hundred*, *thousand*, *million*, and *billion* are expressed as follows:

9	900
3	3,000
4	400,000
8	8,000,000
7	7,000,000,000

NOTE: The *n* for 100 is placed under the number, and the *m* for *million* is placed beside the number; this practice minimizes the possibility of misreading either symbol.

Dollars after a number is expressed by *d*:

1	$1
5	$500
2	$2,000

NOTE: *One* and *two* are written in Arabic numerals when used with abbreviations, addresses, and dates.

Following a number, *cents*, *percent*, and *o'clock* are expressed by a raised *s*, *pr*, and *o* respectively:

6	6 cents
9	9 percent
7	7 o'clock

A sum consisting of dollars and cents is written by raising the figures for the cents and without the *d* for *dollars*:

15 23	$15.23

New phrase: _we think_

New words: _ranged_   _adjourned_   _total_   _fund_   _general_   _evening_   _attended_   _voters_

LESSON 19   Page 56

65-D-6. VOCABULARY PREVIEW OF NEW MATERIAL

Wells, Becky, Walker, with our, January, June, strive, confidence, identify, achieving, reverse, specific, pertinent, information, strict, duplicate (noun), retained, authorize, together, liability, damage, whatsoever, appraisal, evaluating, candidate

LESSON 66

66-A. THE 20-WORD SPRINT

66-B. PREVIEWED NEW DICTATION

Material you previewed in 65-D-6 will be dictated to you.

66-C. THE 350-WORD DASH

19-F. SPEEDFORM ACCELERATOR

In the following plate, 105 words are Speedforms or Speedform related words.

New phrases: to obtain   on these   in order   which is   and return

New words: most   promotions

19-G. PREPARATION FOR LESSON 20

Be able to read 19-A and 19-B at 90 wam; the other plates at 80 wam.

Write each preview outline 3 consecutive times; then write 19-A, 19-B, and 19-C in "double thought" phrases.

LESSON 19   Page 57

65-D-2. WORD SELECTION

principal—highest in rank, main; leader, head of a school; capital sum
principle—basic, fundamental truth; rule of action

NOTE: The following material includes the words presented in Lessons 61-64 as well as those given above.

65-D-3. SPELLING

65-D-4. PHONETIC STUDIES

raping
raping

bãr
bãr

kil
kil

sē
sē

ãr
ãr

65-D-5. DERIVATIVE DEVELOPMENT

LESSON 65 — Page 190

LESSON 20

● **20-A. NOTETAKING CONCENTRATION
(LESSONS 1-17)**

Strive for quick, fluent writing of outlines.

● **20-B. NOTETAKING CONCENTRATION
(LESSONS 1-18)**

65-D. PREPARATION FOR LESSON 66

Continue with the same pattern of study as in the previous lessons.

65-D-1. PUNCTUATION

Rule 20. Spell out street names that are numbers up to twelve. State house numbers in figures except for house number One. If a street number follows a house number, it is sometimes written 181 - 15 Street or 181 Fifteenth Street.

Send the letter to One Ninth Avenue.
The main office is at 2 South 13th Street.

▶ NOTE: The following notes require the application of Rules 16-19 as well as that given above.

20-C. NOTETAKING CONCENTRATION (LESSONS 1-19)

20-D. PREPARATION FOR LESSON 21

Be able to read the notes in 20-A, 20-B, and 20-C at no less than 80 words a minute.

Write the notes in "double thought" phrases.

64-D-6. VOCABULARY PREVIEW OF NEW MATERIAL

announce, appointment, assist, Supreme, Duplicating, Products, King, Printers, Lithographers, Hudson, Frank, Daniel, skillful, application, continue, capacity, in the past, seeking, policies, identical, established, sincere, thanks, welcome, ensuring, we have been able, to provide, prior

LESSON 65

65-A. THE 15-WORD SPRINT

65-B. PREVIEWED NEW DICTATION

Material you previewed in 64-D-6 will be dictated to you.

65-C. THE 350-WORD DASH

LESSON 65   Page 188

LESSON 21

21-A. RECAP OF LESSON 19

New phrases: _____ we have been able _____ it will not be _____ cannot be

New words: _____ labor _____ finishing _____ often _____ promote _____ occupancy _____ charge _____ foundation _____ noise _____ large _____ display _____ met _____ placement _____ salaries _____ laborers _____ laboratory _____ main _____ ceremonies _____ enjoy _____ indicated _____ citizens _____ agricultural _____ hall (haul) _____ inquired _____ officials _____ both

LESSON 21

Page 60

64-D-2. WORD SELECTION

interstate—between states
intrastate—within a state

NOTE: These notes also include words presented in Lessons 60-63.

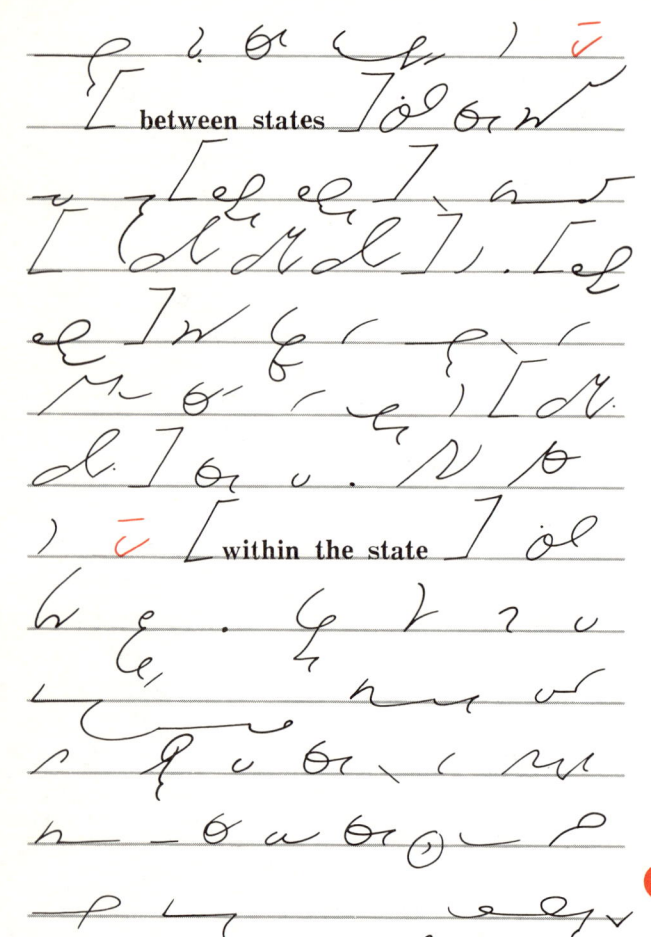

64-D-3. SPELLING

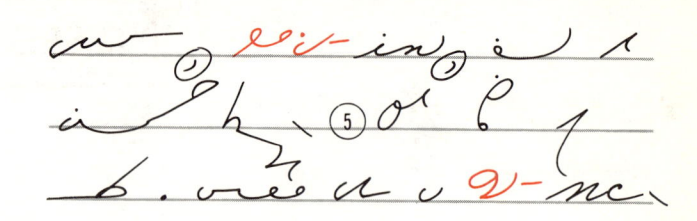

64-D-4. PHONETIC STUDIES

sōl
sōl

pēs
pēs

medl
medl

prā
prā

mēt
mēt

64-D-5. DERIVATIVE DEVELOPMENT

LESSON 64
Page 187

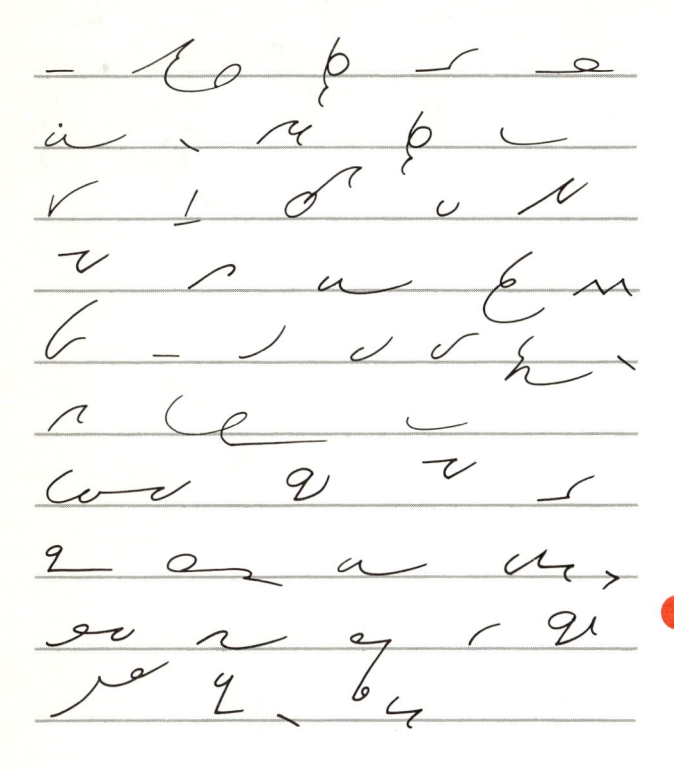

21-B. THE COMPOUND ELEMENT OVER

Sound(s) of	Shorthand Stroke(s)	Longhand Word(s)
ōvər	(disjoined)	over
ōvərchärj		overcharge
ōvərlukt		overlooked
ōvərsīt		oversight

▶ NOTE: The compound element *over* is indicated by a disjoined *o* stroke above the line.

New words: account removed error address prizes

21-C. THE WORD BEGINNING AL-

Sound(s) of	Shorthand Stroke(s)	Longhand Word(s)
ôl-		
ôlmōst		almost
ôlredē		already
ôlthō		although
ôlwāz		always

▶ NOTE: The word beginning *al-* has the sound of *ôl-* and is expressed by the *o* stroke.

New phrase: to finish

New word: doubt proper

LESSON 21   Page 61

64-D. PREPARATION FOR LESSON 65

Follow the same pattern of study that you used in the last lesson.

64-D-1. PUNCTUATION

Rule 19. Use a comma to precede *for instance, namely, viz, i.e.,* and *that is.* These words may be preceded by a semicolon, a colon, or a dash if they precede an enumeration of several items.

The fee, that is, $1, was small.
Sales were high in several areas; namely, Forest Heights, Flower Park, and Golf Manor.

▶ NOTE: In the following paragraph, you will need to apply Rules 15-18 as well as the one presented above.

21-D. REINFORCEMENT

New phrases: to be sure — to do — to miss — Very truly yours (CF)

New words: single — done — annual — whether — also — canvass (canvas) — thorough

21-E. SPEEDFORM ACCELERATOR

87 Speedforms or Speedform related words appear in the following plate.

New words: reasons — arrival — food — maintained — again — points — interview — allowed

21-F. PREPARATION FOR LESSON 22

Be able to read 21-A at 90 wam, the other plates at 80 wam. Write each preview outline 3 consecutive times; then write 21-D and 21-E in "double thought" phrases.

Work for automatic recall of shorthand outlines; remember that you can write shorthand as fast as you can think it!

LESSON 21   Page 62

63-D-6. VOCABULARY PREVIEW OF NEW MATERIAL

extend, features, magazine, earnest, developments, economy, highlight, events, significance (CF), permission, literature, guarantee, similar, nevertheless, minimum, manuscript, compiled, cooperation

LESSON 64

64-A. THE 15-WORD SPRINT

64-B. PREVIEWED NEW DICTATION

Material you previewed in 63-D-6 will be dictated to you.

64-C. THE 300-WORD DASH

LESSON 64

Page 185

LESSON 22

● **22-A. RECAP OF LESSON 21**

New phrases: ⟨shorthand⟩ had been   ⟨shorthand⟩ to have been

New words: ⟨shorthand⟩ sorry   ⟨shorthand⟩ failed   ⟨shorthand⟩ original   ⟨shorthand⟩ mayor   ⟨shorthand⟩ occur   ⟨shorthand⟩ wondering   ⟨shorthand⟩ morning   ⟨shorthand⟩ council (counsel)   ⟨shorthand⟩ extent   ⟨shorthand⟩ nearby   ⟨shorthand⟩ exist   ⟨shorthand⟩ determine   ⟨shorthand⟩ living   ⟨shorthand⟩ occupied   ⟨shorthand⟩ moving   ⟨shorthand⟩ against

LESSON 22   Page 63

63-D-2. WORD SELECTION

adapt—to adjust or make suitable
adept—skillful
adopt—to put into practice as one's own; to accept, as a report; to take by choice into a relationship, as an heir

> **NOTE:** The following notes include the words shown in Lessons 59-62 as well as those presented here.

63-D-3. SPELLING

63-D-4. PHONETIC STUDIES

dāz
dāz

plăn
plăn

văl
văl

thrü
thrü

63-D-5. DERIVATIVE DEVELOPMENT

LESSON 63
Page 184

22-B. THE WORD ENDING -BLE

Sound(s) of	Shorthand Stroke(s)	Longhand Word(s)
-bl		
əvāləbl		available
pāəbl		payable
trubl		trouble

> **NOTE:** The ending *-ble* is expressed by the *b* stroke.

New words: _____ locate _____ before _____ lose _____ valuable

22-C. THE WORD BEGINNING CON-

Sound(s) of	Shorthand Stroke(s)	Longhand Word(s)
kon-, kən-		
konfərəns		conference
kənsümər		consumer
kəntinū		continue

> **NOTE:** The beginning *con-* is expressed by joining the *k* and *n* strokes.

22-D. THE WORD BEGINNING COM-

Sound(s) of	Shorthand Stroke(s)	Longhand Word(s)
kom-, kəm-		
kəmérshəl		commercial
kəmpãr		compare
kompətishən		competition
kəmplēt		complete

> **NOTE:** The sounds of the beginning *com-* are expressed by joining the *k* and *m* strokes.

22-E. REINFORCEMENT

New words: _____ notes _____ solving

LESSON 22   Page 64

63-D. PREPARATION FOR LESSON 64

As before, follow the same pattern of study that you have been using.

63-D-1. PUNCTUATION

Rule 18. Spell out names of states unless accompanied by cities. Do not abbreviate such titles as Governor, Professor, etc., when they precede only the last names of persons. An abbreviation may be written without punctuation when used as a symbol for the name of an organization. Spell out units of measure, unless they occur frequently, such as in tabulations or invoices.

While in Pennsylvania, Governor Williams spoke on the new FDA policies.
The picnic committee purchased 10 pounds of hamburger and 5 gallons of lemonade.

> **NOTE:** The following material includes application of Rules 14-17 as well as the one above.

22-F. MODIFIED ALPHABETIC STROKE, ld

Sound(s) of	Shorthand Stroke(s)	Longhand Word(s)
ld		
bild		build
fōldərs		folders
ōld		old
wėrld		world

▶ **NOTE:** The *ld* bend is expressed by swinging the *l* stroke up at its end.

New phrases: to build — since the
New words: system — storage

22-G. SPEEDFORM ACCELERATOR

73 Speedforms or Speedform related words appear below.

New phrase: you may

New words: remember — inventory — lower

22-H. PREPARATION FOR LESSON 23

Be able to read 22-A at 90 wam, the other plates at 80 wam. Write each preview outline 3 consecutive times; then write 22-A and 22-G in "double thought" phrases.

LESSON 22
Page 65

62-D-5. DERIVATIVE DEVELOPMENT

62-D-6. VOCABULARY PREVIEW OF NEW MATERIAL

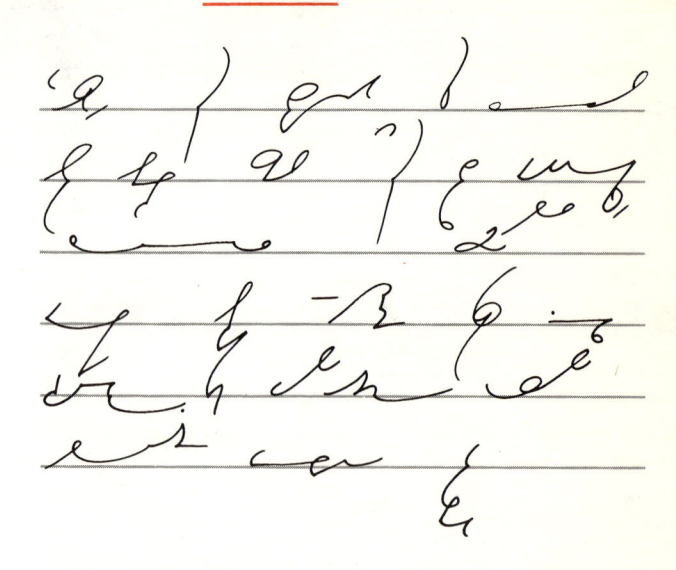

supervised, graduate, assistants, greatly, eminently, it has been, techniques, actively, undergraduate, especially, qualified, elementary, secondary, collegiate, textbook, introduction, bible, himself, counseling, audio-visual, radio, television, semester, speakers

LESSON 63

63-A. THE 15-WORD SPRINT

63-B. PREVIEWED NEW DICTATION

You will take the new material that you previewed in 62-D-6.

63-C. THE 300-WORD DASH

LESSON 63   Page 182

LESSON 23

23-A RECAP OF LESSON 22

New phrases: at them, to become, you would be able, that you (that your)

New words: perhaps, Larry, elimination, between, collected, commissioner, possibly, tax, collection, same, might, forth

23-B. COMBINED ALPHABETIC STROKES, *dm, dn*

Sound(s) of	Shorthand Stroke(s)	Longhand Word(s)
dim, dən, dn		
aksədənt		accident
dimanding		demanding
prezədənt		president
stüdnt		student

NOTE: The *dm, dn* bend is expressed by combining the *d* and *m* strokes in a long upward curve to the left.

New word: further

LESSON 23 Page 66

62-D-2. WORD SELECTION

eraser—the implement with which one removes copy
erasure—the act of removing copy; the place from which copy has been removed

> **NOTE:** These notes include words presented in Lessons 58–61 as well as those given above.

62-D-3. SPELLING

62-D-4. PHONETIC STUDIES

kėrnl
kėrnl

disēst
dəzēzd

sēn
sēn

rōd
rōd

bôrn
bôrn

LESSON 62

Page 181

23-C. THE WORD ENDINGS -CHER, -TURE

Sound(s) of	Shorthand Stroke(s)	Longhand Word(s)
-chər, -chùr	(disjoined)	
fēchər		feature
fėrnəchər		furniture
məchùr		mature
tēchər		teacher

▶ NOTE: The word endings -cher, -ture are expressed by a disjoined ch stroke.

New word: natural

23-D. REINFORCEMENT

New words: explanation   cause
demonstrate (CF)   matter
reached   wage   future

23-E. THE WORD ENDINGS -ER, -OR IN SPEEDFORM RELATED WORDS AND CONTRACTED FORMS

Shorthand Stroke(s)	Longhand Word(s)
(disjoined)	
	contractor
	demonstrator
	director
	greater
	manufacturers

▶ NOTE: The word endings -er, -or in Speedform related words and Contracted Forms are expressed by a disjoined r stroke.

23-F. GEOGRAPHICAL LOCATIONS

Chicago, Illinois (IL)
Detroit, Michigan (MI)
Los Angeles, California (CA)
Philadelphia, Pennsylvania (PA)

New phrase: who was

LESSON 23   Page 67

62-D. PREPARATION FOR LESSON 63

Follow the same pattern of study that you used in the last lesson.

62-D-1. PUNCTUATION

Rule 17. Hyphenate a compound adjective if used before a noun.

She is a well-mannered secretary.

▶ NOTE: In the notes on the following page, you will need to apply Rules 13-16 as well as the one given above.

LESSON 62   Page 180

23-G. SPEEDFORM ACCELERATOR

85 Speedforms or Speedform related words appear below.

New phrases: it would   he could

New words: idea   manual   clause   section   accuracy   oppose   upon   editor

23-H. REINFORCEMENT

New phrase: to purchase

New word: included

23-I. PREPARATION FOR LESSON 24

Be able to read 23-A at 90 wam, the other plates at 80 wam. Write each preview outline 3 consecutive times; then write 23-A and 23-G in "double thought" phrases.

LESSON 23   **Page 68**

thrōn
thrōn

profit
profit

61-D-5. DERIVATIVE DEVELOPMENT

61-D-6. VOCABULARY PREVIEW OF NEW MATERIAL

Patterson, Hicks, dozen, recipe, referred, assembled, discount, furnish, boxes, Peters, Huntington, contents, bookstores, various, universities, inquire, campus, I am sure, catalog, descriptive, students

LESSON 62

62-A. THE 15-WORD SPRINT

62-B. PREVIEWED NEW DICTATION

Material you previewed in 61-D-6 will be dictated to you.

62-C. THE 300-WORD DASH

LESSON 62   Page 179

LESSON 24

24-A. RECAP OF LESSON 23

New phrases: you might, who is, they can, they have not

New words: unhappy, let, semesters, position, body, pictures, complaint, agents, customers, appointed, handled

24-B. THE WORD ENDINGS -ACLE, -ICAL, -ICLE

Sound(s) of	Shorthand Stroke(s)	Longhand Word(s)
-əkl	(disjoined)	
ärtəkl		article
kritəkl		critical
medəkl		medical
mirəkl		miracle
praktəkl		practical

NOTE: The endings *-acle, -ical, -icle* are expressed by a disjoined *k* stroke.

New words: seen (scene), appeared, sound, cures

LESSON 24   Page 69

61-D-2. WORD SELECTION

cite—calling upon authoritatively to appear, as before a court; quoting authority or proof

sight—a view; the power of seeing; a small device through which objects are to be seen

site—local position, as of a town; place or scene of anything

▶ **NOTE:** The following notes include the words presented in Lessons 57-60 as well as those given above.

61-D-3. SPELLING

61-D-4. PHONETIC STUDIES

vān
vān

stāk
stāk

märshəl
märshəl

LESSON 61   Page 178

24-C. SHORTHAND ALPHABET

Sound(s) of	Shorthand Stroke(s)	Longhand Word(s)
y	◌	
biyond		beyond
milyən		million
əpinyən		opinion
yung		young

NOTE: The sound of *y* is written with a small circle. The sound of *yo* is written with the *y* and *o* strokes. The sound of *yu* is written with the *u* stroke.

MODIFIED Y:

ya	(loop *a*)	
yärd		yard
ye	(loop *e*)	
yes		yes
yī	(loop *ī*)	
yīping		yiping

NOTE: The sounds of *ya, ye, yi* are written by combining the *y* stroke and the vowel stroke into a loop.

New phrases: to find — would not be

New words: bowl — dogs — yet — drop — youth — yelled — overcome — year — workers — holding — bureau

24-D. REINFORCEMENT

New phrase: some of the

New words: farm — classes — conclusions — logical — egg — yolks — field

LESSON 24 — Page 70

61-D. PREPARATION FOR LESSON 62

Continue the pattern of study that you have been using.

61-D-1. PUNCTUATION

Rule 16. Use a comma to set off a phrase denoting residence when it is used with the name of a person. Use a comma to separate the parts of addresses, dates, and geographical names.

Your request was from Mr. King, of Boise, Idaho.
About May 1, 19--, we lived in a house at 1893 Valley View, Bismarck, North Dakota.

▶ **NOTE:** The notes on the following page require applications of Rules 12-15 as well as the one above.

24-E. GEOGRAPHICAL LOCATIONS

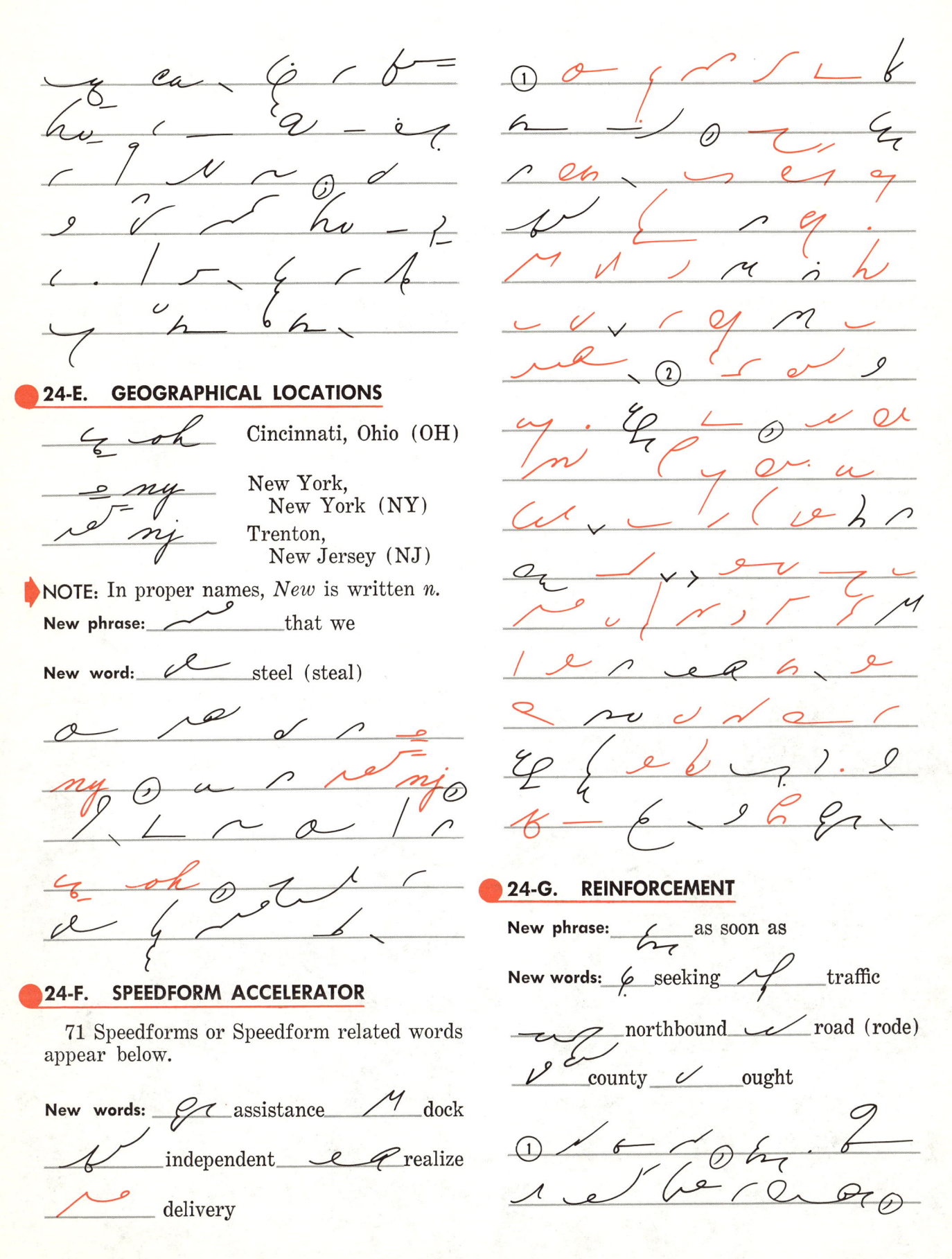

oh   Cincinnati, Ohio (OH)

ny   New York, New York (NY)

nj   Trenton, New Jersey (NJ)

NOTE: In proper names, *New* is written *n*.

New phrase: _____ that we

New word: _____ steel (steal)

24-F. SPEEDFORM ACCELERATOR

71 Speedforms or Speedform related words appear below.

New words: _____ assistance   _____ dock

_____ independent   _____ realize

_____ delivery

24-G. REINFORCEMENT

New phrase: _____ as soon as

New words: _____ seeking   _____ traffic

_____ northbound   _____ road (rode)

_____ county   _____ ought

LESSON 24   Page 71

wēk
wēk

60-D-5. DERIVATIVE DEVELOPMENT

60-D-6. VOCABULARY PREVIEW OF NEW MATERIAL

Stone, to thank you for the, educators, community, younger, generation, civic, unexpected, services, equipped, staffed, to provide, everything, modern, banking, window, evening, parking, boxes, depository, central, upon, you will find, eager

LESSON 61

61-A. THE 15-WORD SPRINT

61-B. PREVIEWED NEW DICTATION

Material you previewed in 60-D-6 will be dictated to you.

61-C. THE 300-WORD DASH

LESSON 61   Page 176

24-H. PREPARATION FOR LESSON 25

Be able to read 24-A at 90 wam, the other plates at 80 wam.

Write each preview outline 3 consecutive times; then write 24-D, 24-F, and 24-G in "double-thought" phrases.

LESSON 25

25-A. RECAP OF LESSON 24

New phrases: Dear Mr. (CF) Dear Mrs. (CF) must have Yours very truly (CF) for his

New words: skill overall strike went bright yielded relations packaging drawn Ames Mr. (CF) Cordially (CF) appointees trends current desirable Smith appreciation chief growing area

LESSON 25 Page 72

60-D-2. WORD SELECTION

complementary—serving to fill out or complete

complimentary—expressive of regard; of the nature of or containing a compliment

> **NOTE:** The following notes contain the words presented in Lessons 56-59 as well as those given here.

60-D-3. SPELLING

60-D-4. PHONETIC STUDIES

sēling
sēling

blü
blü
blü

strāt
strāt

gest
gest

LESSON 60   Page 175

25-B. THE WORD ENDING -FUL

Sound(s) of	Shorthand Stroke(s)	Longhand Word(s)
-fəl		
būtəfəl		beautiful
kãrfəl		careful
ūsfəl		useful

NOTE: The ending *-ful* is expressed by the *f* stroke.

New words: built

successful   engineering

designer

60-D. PREPARATION FOR LESSON 61

Follow the same pattern of study that you used in the preceding lesson.

60-D-1. PUNCTUATION

Rule 15. Use a comma to separate two consecutive parallel adjectives modifying a single noun.

A long, complicated opinion was read.

NOTE: The following material includes Rules 11-14 as well as this one.

25-C. THE WORD ENDINGS -CASION, -CATION

Sound(s) of	Shorthand Stroke(s)	Longhand Word(s)
-kāshən, -kāzhən	(disjoined)	
lōkāshən		location
əkāzhən		occasion
vākāshən		vacation

▶ NOTE: A disjoined combination of the *k* and *n* strokes represents the word endings *-casion*, *-cation*.

New words: publication   earned   Yiddish

25-D. THE WORD ENDINGS -SATION, -ZATION

Sound(s) of	Shorthand Stroke(s)	Longhand Word(s)
-sāshən, -zāshən	(disjoined)	
ôthərəzāshən		authorization
kompənsāshən		compensation
stābləzāshən		stabilization

▶ NOTE: The disjoined combination of the *s* and *n* strokes is used for the sounds of *-sation*, *-zation*.

New words: adequate   speaker

25-E. THE WORD ENDING -INGS

Sound(s) of	Shorthand Stroke(s)	Longhand Word(s)
-ingz	(disjoined)	
bildingz		buildings
ėrningz		earnings
mētingz		meetings

▶ NOTE: The ending *-ings* is expressed by a disjoined combination of the *ng* and *s* strokes.

New words: concerned   things   mailings   federal   administrator   center

LESSON 25   Page 74

59-D-6. VOCABULARY PREVIEW OF NEW MATERIAL

Warren, volume, particular, manufacturer, unusual, practically, executive, grown, exploiting, enormous, valuable, within the, you will find, chemicals, textiles, import, export, petroleum, automotive, digest, trends, taxation, wages, significant (CF), forecast, data, subscribe, outstanding, journal

LESSON 60

60-A. THE 15-WORD SPRINT

60-B. PREVIEWED NEW DICTATION

Your teacher will dictate material you previewed in 59-D-6.

60-C. THE 300-WORD DASH

New word: _____ f.o.b.

LESSON 60   Page 173

25-F. GEOGRAPHICAL LOCATIONS

Boston, Massachusetts (MA)

Houston, Texas (TX)

San Francisco, California (CA)

New word: shipment

25-G. REINFORCEMENT

New phrases: in those who want

from those how many

New words: fully helpful applications discount approval comments

25-H. PRECISION PRACTICE

The greater your writing precision, the easier it will be to read your notes. Observe the outlines in color below. Those in the 4 "pairs" could be mistaken for each other if written in poor proportion. Write each of the "pairs" 3 times; then write the sentence twice.

25-I. PREPARATION FOR LESSON 26

Follow the same pattern for Lesson 26 as for Lesson 25, using 25-A and 25-G for "double thought" phrase writing.

59-D-2. WORD SELECTION

leased—conveyed to another by a lease
least—smallest, shortest; in the lower degree

▶ NOTE: These notes include words presented in Lessons 55-58 as well as those given above.

59-D-3. SPELLING

59-D-4. PHONETIC STUDIES

bēch
bēch

wāst
wāst

rōl
rōl

kanvəs
kanvəs

mīnər
mīnər

59-D-5. DERIVATIVE DEVELOPMENT

LESSON 26

26-A. RECAP OF LESSON 25

New phrases: ⎯ less than ⎯ in these ⎯ for these

New words: ⎯ attempts ⎯ homes ⎯ Brown ⎯ series ⎯ lakeside ⎯ durable ⎯ basic ⎯ reduce

26-B. THE WORD ENDINGS -IVE, -SIVE, -TIVE

Sound(s) of	Shorthand Stroke(s)	Longhand Word(s)
-iv, -siv, -tiv	(disjoined)	
komprihensiv		comprehensive
kōopərātiv		cooperative
eksesiv		excessive
egzekūtiv		executive
relətiv		relative

▶ **NOTE:** The endings *-ive, -sive, -tive* are expressed by a disjoined *v,w* stroke close to the preceding stroke.

59-D. PREPARATION FOR LESSON 60

The exercises are of the same type as in the last lesson; follow a similar pattern of study. Remember that your objective is twofold: to expand your shorthand vocabulary and to speed your recall.

59-D-1. PUNCTUATION

Rule 14. Use a comma to set off an introductory participial phrase.

Acknowledging our mistake, we are apologizing.

▶ **NOTE:** Rules 10-13 should be applied as well as the one above.

New phrase: [shorthand] could be

New words: [shorthand] representative
[shorthand] prospective (CF) [shorthand] expensive
[shorthand] mind [shorthand] employees
[shorthand] wrong [shorthand] assume [shorthand] spirit

26-C. GEOGRAPHICAL LOCATIONS

[shorthand] Pittsburgh, Pennsylvania (PA)
[shorthand] Shreveport, Louisiana (LA)
[shorthand] St. Louis, Missouri (MO)
[shorthand] Washington, D.C. (DC)

NOTE: In proper names, -port is expressed by p-t; -burgh (-burg, -berg), by b; and St., by s-t.

New words: [shorthand] effective [shorthand] connection

26-D. THE WORD ENDINGS -ETY, -ITY

Sound(s) of	Shorthand Stroke(s)	Longhand Word(s)
-ətē	[shorthand] (disjoined)	
kəpasətē	[shorthand]	capacity
kəmūnətē	[shorthand]	community
fəsilətē	[shorthand]	facility
sikūrətē	[shorthand]	security
səsīətē	[shorthand]	society

NOTE: The endings -ety, -ity are expressed by a disjoined combination of the t and e strokes.

New phrase: [shorthand] to insure

New words: [shorthand] visitors [shorthand] sufficient
[shorthand] protection [shorthand] automobile

LESSON 26 — Page 77

58-D-5. DERIVATIVE DEVELOPMENT

58-D-6. VOCABULARY PREVIEW OF NEW MATERIAL

convention, scheduled (CF), New Orleans, extend, wishes, successful, lunch, physical, facilities, cordial, preview, brochure, function, accommodated, centrally, located, ample, parking, downtown, forward

LESSON 59

59-A. THE 15-WORD SPRINT

59-B. PREVIEWED NEW DICTATION
Material you previewed in 58-D-6 will be dictated to you.

59-C. THE 300-WORD DASH

LESSON 59   Page 170

26-E. THE WORD ENDING -TUAL

Sound(s) of	Shorthand Stroke(s)	Longhand Word(s)
-chŭəl	(disjoined)	
akchŭəl		actual
mūchŭəl		mutual

NOTE: The ending *-tual* is expressed by a disjoined *l* stroke.

New words: professor, typical, review, recommended

26-F. REINFORCEMENT

New phrase: we shall not

New words: assumption, Civic, customary, performance, worries, crowds

26-G. PRECISION PRACTICE

The following 4 "pairs" of outlines could be misread if written in poor proportion. Write each "pair" 3 times; then write the sentence twice.

26-H. PREPARATION FOR LESSON 27

Follow the same pattern for Lesson 27 as for Lesson 26, using 26-A and 26-F for "double thought" phrase writing.

LESSON 26 — Page 78

The reason was not given, although I had asked for it.
She gave no reason, for everyone understood.

▶ **NOTE:** Rules 9-12 must be applied as well as Rule 13.

▶ **58-D-2. WORD SELECTION**

advice—recommendation
advise—to recommend or counsel

▶ **NOTE:** The following paragraph includes words presented in Lessons 54-57 as well as those given above.

▶ **58-D-3. SPELLING**

▶ **58-D-4. PHONETIC STUDIES**

herd
herd

rīt
rīt
rīt

nō
nō

rezədənts
rezədəns

LESSON 58   **Page 169**

LESSON 27

27-A. RECAP OF LESSON 26

New phrases: ___ one of our ___ to turn ___ by those

New words: ___ residential ___ afford ___ expert ___ country ___ estate ___ incomplete ___ property ___ farmers ___ similar ___ university ___ Johnson ___ uncertain ___ ago ___ protect ___ attractive

LESSON 27 — Page 79

LESSON 58

58-A. THE 15-WORD SPRINT

58-B. PREVIEWED NEW DICTATION

Material you previewed in 57-D-6 will be dictated to you.

58-C. THE 300-WORD DASH

58-D. PREPARATION FOR LESSON 59

Continue the same pattern of study as in the previous lesson.

58-D-1. PUNCTUATION

Rule 13. Use a comma to separate from the main clause a clause of reason introduced by *for* or *as* and a clause of concession introduced by *though* or *although*.

27-B. THE WORD BEGINNING SUB-

Sound(s) of	Shorthand Stroke(s)	Longhand Word(s)
səb-, sub-		
səbmit		submit
subsəkwənt		subsequent
səbstanshəl		substantial

▶ NOTE: The *s* stroke is used for the beginning *sub-*.

New words: mine, preparation, treatment, assets, different, percentage

27-C. THE WORD ENDINGS -SCRIBE, -SCRIPT

Sound(s) of	Shorthand Stroke(s)	Longhand Word(s)
-skrīb	(disjoined)	
-skript	(disjoined)	
diskrīb		describe
pōstskript		postscript
səbskrīb		subscribe

▶ NOTE: The ending *-scribe* is expressed by a disjoined combination of the *s* and *b* strokes; *-script*, by a disjoined combination of the *s* and *p* strokes.

New phrase: for the past

New words: endorsement, magazine, subscription

LESSON 27

57-D-3. SPELLING

57-D-4. PHONETIC STUDIES

əsent
əsent

fãr
fãr

hōl
hōl

ad
ad

sēz
sēs

57-D-5. DERIVATIVE DEVELOPMENT

57-D-6. VOCABULARY PREVIEW OF NEW MATERIAL

Nichols, overdue, courtesy, urging, explanation, whatever, frankly, reluctant, legal, collection, hesitate, direction, unpleasant, expensive, unless, alternative, institute, proceedings, won't

LESSON 57 Page 167

27-D. GEOGRAPHICAL LOCATIONS

Baltimore, Maryland (MD)
Milwaukee, Wisconsin (WI)
Minneapolis, Minnesota (MN)

New words: chapter   once

27-E. REINFORCEMENT

New phrases: we have not   to follow   to this

New words: gone   American   entitled   local   wonderful   exciting   consistently   exchange

27-F. PRECISION PRACTICE

Write the red outlines 3 times each, being careful of proportion; then write each sentence twice.

27-G. PREPARATION FOR LESSON 28

Continue the same pattern of study as for Lesson 27, using 27-A and 27-E for "double thought" phrase writing.

LESSON 27   **Page 81**

57-D. PREPARATION FOR LESSON 58

Follow the same pattern of study that you used in the last lesson.

57-D-1. PUNCTUATION

Rule 12. Use a comma to set off an introductory adverbial phrase containing a verb. Use a comma to set off an introductory phrase that does not contain a verb if a pause would be made at that point in reading or if a comma at that point is essential for emphasis or clarity.

In order to be on time, we must leave by one o'clock.
After the special action on July 1, we voted no additional changes.

> NOTE: In the following paragraph, you will need to apply Rules 8-11 as well as the one given above.

57-D-2. WORD SELECTION

council—a group of people called together for conference, consultation, or advice
counsel—advice or deliberation; exchanging of ideas; person who gives legal advice

> NOTE: The following notes include words shown in Lessons 53-56 as well as those given above.

LESSON 57   Page 166

LESSON 28

● **28-A. RECAP OF LESSON 27**

New phrase: _____ who have not

New words: _____ larger _____ choices _____ subscribers _____ sold _____ growth _____ readers _____ overflowing

● **28-B. RECAP OF LESSONS 21-26**

New phrase: _____ from that

New words: _____ conducted _____ stop _____ physical _____ agency _____ survey _____ claims _____ Owen _____ won't

LESSON 28 — Page 82

LESSON 57

57-A. THE 15-WORD SPRINT

57-B. PREVIEWED NEW DICTATION

Your instructor will dictate material that includes the new words and phrases which you previewed in 56-D-6.

57-C. THE 300-WORD DASH

New word: mathematically (CF)

New phrase: ___ had not been

New words: ___ acceptable ___ concert ___ budget ___ unable ___ considerable

New phrase: ___ at least

New words: ___ proposal ___ source ___ extra ___ military ___ schedule(CF) ___ western ___ veterans ___ motor ___ units ___ vehicles ___ heard ___ haven't ___ toward

LESSON 28 Page 83

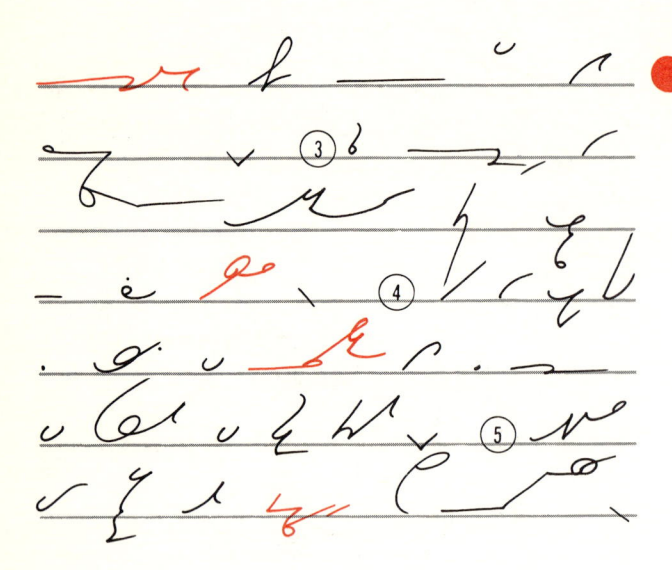

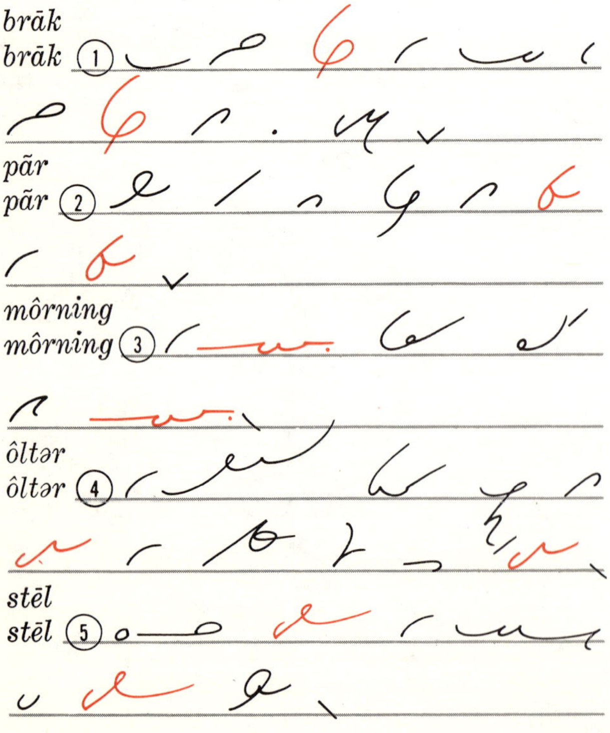

56-D-5. DERIVATIVE DEVELOPMENT

Derivatives of five Speedforms are shown; write each outline 3 times consecutively, saying it as you write. Then transcribe the sentences. The derivatives used are in color.

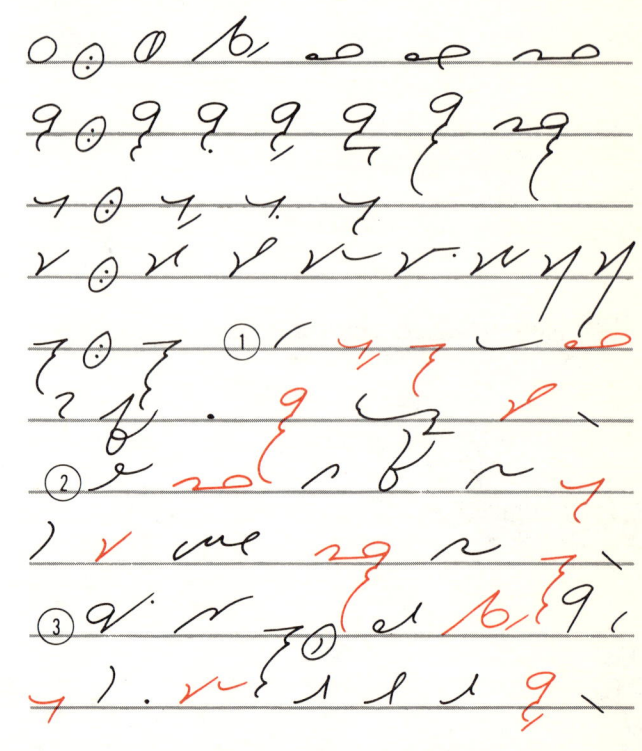

56-D-4. PHONETIC STUDIES

Words which are different in meaning and spelling but are alike in pronunciation and shorthand form are shown below in phonetic form. Note that, in some cases, they are the same part of speech, while in others, they are different. Transcribe the sentences, selecting the proper spelling in each instance for the outlines shown in color.

brăk
brăk ①

pãr
pãr ②

môrning
môrning ③

ôltər
ôltər ④

stēl
stēl ⑤

56-D-6. VOCABULARY PREVIEW OF NEW MATERIAL

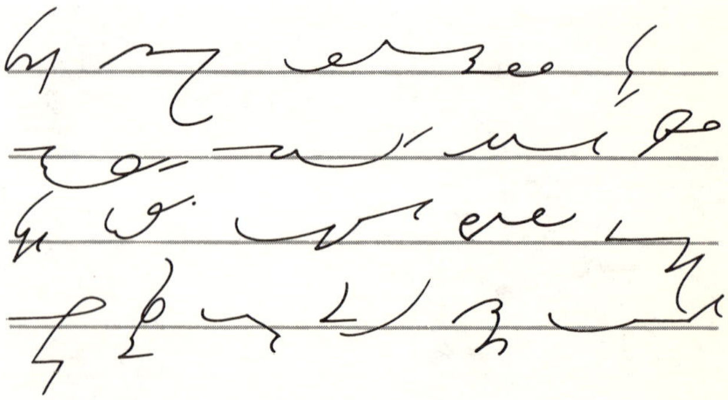

beautiful, tumbler, revolutionary, picked, insulated, molded, walls, tiny, pockets, sweating, liquids, exterior, comfortable, magnificent (CF), fraction, rings, furniture, thank you for your, limits

LESSON 56

New phrases: to fill   Dear Ms. (CF)

New words: gasoline   honest   circumstances (CF)   town   per   campaign   donated   enable   women   Green   trucks   fuel   never   tanks   thus   clothing   minimum   venture

28-C. GEOGRAPHICAL LOCATIONS

Atlanta, Georgia (GA)
Jackson, Mississippi (MS)
Phoenix, Arizona (AZ)
San Diego, California (CA)

New words: description   hard

28-D. PRECISION PRACTICE

As with other exercises, write 3 times the outlines that differ in proportion; then write each sentence twice.

28-E. PREPARATION FOR LESSON 29

Continue the same pattern of study as for previous lessons; this time write all of the plates in "double thought" phrases.

LESSON 28   Page 84

56-D. PREPARATION FOR LESSON 57

In the next ten lessons, you will continue the review of punctuation rules, word selection, and spelling. Two new exercises will also appear, one in Phonetic Studies, and one in Derivative Development. The directions for the familiar exercises will continue the same. Directions for the two new exercises will be given at the time each first appears in this lesson.

56-D-1. PUNCTUATION

Rule 11. Use a comma to set off words in apposition.

Our representative, Senator Ware, is in town.

> NOTE: In the following paragraph, you will need to apply Rules 7-10 as well as the one given above.

56-D-2. WORD SELECTION

stationary—fixed, not movable
stationery—paper on which letters are written

> NOTE: The following notes include words presented in Lessons 52-55 as well as those given above.

New word: architect (CF)

56-D-3. SPELLING

LESSON 56   Page 163

LESSON 29

29-A. RECAP OF LESSON 28

New phrases: we may — of many — before the — Yours truly (CF)

New words: gallons — still — sizeable — force — purchaser — taxpayers — amazing — rapid — installation — treasury — temporary — appraisal — entertainment — type — hundreds — majority — base — production — progress

LESSON 56

56-A. THE TEN-WORD SPRINT

56-B. PREVIEWED NEW DICTATION

Material you previewed in 55-D-4 will be dictated to you.

56-C. THE 300-WORD DASH

LESSON 56

Page 162

29-C. THE WORD ENDINGS -OUS, -US

Sound(s) of	Shorthand Stroke(s)	Longhand Word(s)
-əs	(disjoined)	
bōnəs		bonus
kampəs		campus
prēvēəs		previous
trimendəs		tremendous
vāreəs		various

▶ NOTE: The word endings *-ous,-us* are expressed by a disjoined *s* stroke.

New phrase: she will

New words: possibilities, shop, plus, secretarial, unsatisfactory, small, limited, savings

29-B. THE WORD ENDING -BILITY

Sound(s) of	Shorthand Stroke(s)	Longhand Word(s)
-bilətē	(disjoined)	
əbilətē		ability
kāpəbilətē		capability
līəbilətē		liability

▶ NOTE: The word ending *-bility* is represented by the disjoined *b* stroke.

New words: responsibility, duties, literature

LESSON 29

Page 86

55-D-4. VOCABULARY PREVIEW OF NEW MATERIAL

proposed, inclusion, biographical, dictionary, questionnaire, editorial, particular, be sure, nominations, sources, duplication, inevitable, university, degree, granted, positions, major, honors, awards, fellowships, publications, limitations, noteworthy, dependent, subscription, criteria, themselves, puts

55-D-5. TRANSCRIPTION TIPS

LESSON 55   Page 161

29-D. REINFORCEMENT

New phrases: ⟨ ⟩ to pass　⟨ ⟩ it would be

New words: ⟨ ⟩ recommendations　⟨ ⟩ principal (principle)　⟨ ⟩ vice　⟨ ⟩ administrative　⟨ ⟩ earliest　⟨ ⟩ academic　⟨ ⟩ authorized　⟨ ⟩ faculty　⟨ ⟩ rather　⟨ ⟩ urge　⟨ ⟩ tests　⟨ ⟩ calendar　⟨ ⟩ Christmas　⟨ ⟩ hesitate　⟨ ⟩ instructor　⟨ ⟩ instead

29-E. GEOGRAPHICAL LOCATIONS

⟨ ⟩ Buffalo, New York (NY)
⟨ ⟩ Kansas City, Missouri (MO)
⟨ ⟩ St. Paul, Minnesota (MN)

New phrase: ⟨ ⟩ to favor

New words: ⟨ ⟩ furnished　⟨ ⟩ I'm

29-F. PRECISION PRACTICE

29-G. PREPARATION FOR LESSON 30

Follow the customary pattern of study, using 29-A for "double thought" phrase writing.

LESSON 29　　　Page 87

55-D. PREPARATION FOR LESSON 56

Follow the same procedures as for the immediately preceding lessons.

55-D-1. PUNCTUATION

Rule 10. Use commas to set off words of direct address.

Your coat, Mary, has been torn.

▶ NOTE: You will need to apply Rules 6-9 as well as the one above.

New word: significant (CF)

55-D-2. WORD SELECTION

farther—refers to distance
further—refers to time, quantity, or degree

▶ NOTE: These notes also include words presented in Lessons 51-54.

55-D-3. SPELLING

New word: registered

LESSON 30

● **30-A. RECAP OF LESSON 29**

New phrases: ⟨shorthand⟩ we should be ⟨shorthand⟩ to face ⟨shorthand⟩ after that

New words: ⟨shorthand⟩ profits ⟨shorthand⟩ ideal ⟨shorthand⟩ challenge ⟨shorthand⟩ extension ⟨shorthand⟩ financial ⟨shorthand⟩ corporation ⟨shorthand⟩ revenue ⟨shorthand⟩ premiums ⟨shorthand⟩ church ⟨shorthand⟩ legal ⟨shorthand⟩ reflected ⟨shorthand⟩ coverage ⟨shorthand⟩ insurance ⟨shorthand⟩ policies

① [shorthand outlines]

② [shorthand outlines]

● **30-B. THE WORD ENDING -SHIP**

Sound(s) of	Shorthand Stroke(s)	Longhand Word(s)
-ship	⟩ (disjoined)	
frendship	⟨shorthand⟩	friendship
membərship	⟨shorthand⟩	membership
ōnərship	⟨shorthand⟩	ownership

▶ **NOTE:** The word ending -ship is expressed by a disjoined sh stroke.

New words: ⟨shorthand⟩ wholesale ⟨shorthand⟩ operating ⟨shorthand⟩ largest ⟨shorthand⟩ industrial ⟨shorthand⟩ dinner ⟨shorthand⟩ club ⟨shorthand⟩ beginning ⟨shorthand⟩ finest ⟨shorthand⟩ parks

① [shorthand outlines]

② [shorthand outlines]

③ [shorthand outlines]

LESSON 30   Page 88

LESSON 55

55-A. THE TEN-WORD SPRINT

55-B. PREVIEWED NEW DICTATION

Material you previewed in 54-D-4 will be dictated to you.

55-C-1. THE 100-WORD DASH

55-C-2. THE 200-WORD DASH

30-C. THE WORD ENDINGS -HOOD, -WARD

Sound(s) of	Shorthand Stroke(s)	Longhand Word(s)
-hud, -wərd	(disjoined)	
ôkwərd		awkward
fôrwərd		forward
līklēhŭd		likelihood

NOTE: The word endings *-hood, -ward* are expressed by a disjoined *d* stroke.

New words: benefit   union   downward   live (adj.)

30-D. THE WORD ENDING -JECT

Sound(s) of	Shorthand Stroke(s)	Longhand Word(s)
-jekt, -jikt		
projekt		project
rijekt		reject
subjikt		subject

NOTE: The word ending *-ject* is expressed by combining the *g, j* and *t* strokes.

New words: neighborhood   fourth   quickly   inquiry

30-E. REINFORCEMENT

New words: private   fees   brought   eligible   authority   treasurer

30-F. GEOGRAPHICAL LOCATIONS

Denver, Colorado (CO)
Indianapolis, Indiana (IN)
Seattle, Washington (WA)

LESSON 30

Tucker, fraternity's, jewelry, sterling, silver, possibilities, existing, engraving, initials, anticipate, interval, receipt, sketch, rings, pendants, dozen, initiates, selections, dedicated

54-D-3. SPELLING

54-D-4. VOCABULARY PREVIEW OF NEW MATERIAL

54-D-5. TRANSCRIPTION TIPS

LESSON 54   Page 158

30-G. THE WORD BEGINNINGS TRAN-, TRANS-

Sound(s) of	Shorthand Stroke(s)	Longhand Word(s)
tran-, trans-, tranz-	(disjoined)	
tranzakshən		transaction
transkript		transcript
transfėr		transfer (n,v)
transpərtāshən		transportation

NOTE: The word beginnings *tran-*, *trans-* are expressed by a disjoined *t* stroke written above the line.

New phrase: we should have

New words: analysis fast appropriate (adj) court

30-H. REINFORCEMENT

New phrase: to permit

New words: Carter topics involved maximum penalty appropriate (v)

30-I. PRECISION PRACTICE

30-J. PREPARATION FOR LESSON 31
Follow the suggested pattern of study, using 30-A, 30-E, and 30-H for "double thought" phrase writing.

LESSON 30 — Page 90

54-D-1. PUNCTUATION

Rule 9. Capitalize the first word and all important words in titles of books, periodicals, and articles. Titles of books, booklets, magazines, and newspapers may be typed entirely in capitals, or they may be underlined with only the first word and all important words capitalized.

Have you read the article on new drilling rigs in the latest edition of GLOBAL OIL? If you want to read the best magazine in your field, subscribe to Global Oil.

▶ NOTE: In the following paragraph, you will need to apply Rules 5-8 as well as the one given above.

54-D-2. WORD SELECTION

beside—*by the side of; near; separated from*
besides—*in addition to; other than; moreover*

▶ NOTE: The notes on the following page include the words presented in Lessons 50-53 as well as those above.

54-D. PREPARATION FOR LESSON 55

Continue with the same study procedures that you have been using.

LESSON 54 Page 157

LESSON 31

31-A. RECAP OF LESSON 30

New phrase: you may be able

New words: got, separate (adj), specifications, representation, documents, deposits

31-B. THE COMPOUND ELEMENT *SELF*

Sound(s) of	Shorthand Stroke(s)	Longhand Word(s)
self		
himself		himself
mīself		myself
self eksplənôtōrē		self-explanatory

NOTE: The compound element *self* is expressed by a combination of the *s* and *e* strokes. It is disjoined and raised at the beginning of a word or as a word; joined at the end of a word.

New words: yourself, themselves, maintenance, license, responsible, machine, itself, formula, effectiveness, runs, higher

LESSON 31 — Page 91

LESSON 54

54-A. THE TEN-WORD SPRINT

54-B. PREVIEWED NEW DICTATION
Material you previewed in 53-D-4 will be dictated to you.

54-C-1. THE 100-WORD DASH

54-C-2. THE 200-WORD DASH

31-C. THE WORD ENDINGS -GRAM, -GRAPH

Sound(s) of	Shorthand Stroke(s)	Longhand Word(s)
-graf		
-gram		
mimēəgraf		mimeograph
parəgraf		paragraph
prōgram		program
teləgram		telegram

▶ **NOTE:** The word ending *-graph* is expressed by the *gr* stroke; *-gram*, by combining the *gr* and *m* strokes.

New words: acknowledge, pages, half, messages, seriously, second, provisions, cross

31-D. THE WORD ENDING -ULATE

Sound(s) of	Shorthand Stroke(s)	Longhand Word(s)
-ulāt, -ulāt, -ūlit	(disjoined)	
ärtikūlit		articulate (adj)
kəngrachùlāt		congratulate
regūlāt		regulate
stimūlāt		stimulate

▶ **NOTE:** The word ending *-ulate* is expressed by a disjoined *u* stroke written close to the preceding stroke.

New words: unusual, technical, congratulations, regulation, emergency, regulator, top, replacement, manner, trial

LESSON 31 — Page 92

53-D-3. SPELLING

53-D-4. VOCABULARY PREVIEW OF NEW MATERIAL

Davis, introduces, predictions, sense, sizeable, biggest, toughest, America, comments, pointing, curb, competitive, attaining, cruising, faster, rugged, economical, one of our, demonstrator (CF), proposition

53-D-5. TRANSCRIPTION TIPS

31-E. REINFORCEMENT

New phrases: Cordially yours (CF)

you should   Dear Miss (CF)

New words: repaired   aware   Doyle   fairness

31-F. GEOGRAPHICAL LOCATIONS

Birmingham, Alabama (AL)

Honolulu, Hawaii (HI)

Norfolk, Virginia (VA)

New words: demonstration (CF)

reception   thousands   quite

listeners   radio

31-G. REINFORCEMENT

New phrase: Sincerely yours (CF)

New words: inspection   zone   Harvey   convince

31-H. PRECISION PRACTICE

31-I. PREPARATION FOR LESSON 32

Follow the usual pattern of study, using 31-A, 31-E, and 31-G for "double thought" phrase writing.

LESSON 31

53-D. PREPARATION FOR LESSON 54

Follow the same procedures that you have been directed to use for similar exercises.

53-D-1. PUNCTUATION

Rule 8. Use a comma to set off parenthetical expressions if a definite pause is indicated.

You haven't, in my opinion, made a very good choice this time.

▶ NOTE: In the following paragraph you will need to apply Rules 4-7 as well as the one given above.

53-D-2. WORD SELECTION

capital—a chief city; money or assets; uppercase letter

capitol—the building or buildings housing legislative bodies (capitalized when it refers to a specific capitol building)

▶ NOTE: The following notes include words presented in Lessons 49-52 as well as those given above.

LESSON 53

Page 154

LESSON 32

32-A. RECAP OF LESSON 31

New phrases: ⟨sh⟩ as you can ⟨sh⟩ to prepare

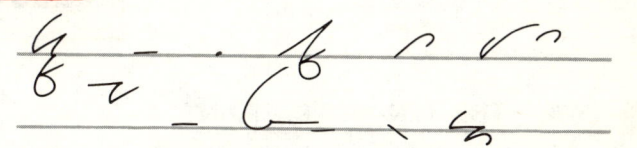

New words: ⟨sh⟩ participate ⟨sh⟩ quote ⟨sh⟩ cooperation ⟨sh⟩ amendment ⟨sh⟩ learn ⟨sh⟩ qualified ⟨sh⟩ district ⟨sh⟩ rental ⟨sh⟩ damage ⟨sh⟩ debate ⟨sh⟩ prove ⟨sh⟩ weather ⟨sh⟩ land ⟨sh⟩ law

32-B. COMBINED ALPHABETIC STROKES, ia, io, iu

Sound(s) of	Shorthand Stroke(s)	Longhand Word(s)
īa, īo, īu	⟨sh⟩	
dīamətər	⟨sh⟩	diameter
priôrətē	⟨sh⟩	priority
trīumf	⟨sh⟩	triumph

NOTE: Phonetic long *i* followed by a basic vowel is expressed by the *i* stroke with a dot inside.

New words: ⟨sh⟩ estimate ⟨sh⟩ it's ⟨sh⟩ urgent ⟨sh⟩ financing ⟨sh⟩ water ⟨sh⟩ drainage ⟨sh⟩ separate (v) ⟨sh⟩ conversation

LESSON 32   Page 94

LESSON 53

53-A. THE TEN-WORD SPRINT

53-B. PREVIEWED NEW DICTATION
You will take dictation including the words and phrases previewed in 52-D-4.

53-C-1. THE 100-WORD DASH

53-C-2. THE 200-WORD DASH

32-C. THE WORD BEGINNING *IM-*

Sound(s) of	Shorthand Stroke(s)	Longhand Word(s)
im-	→	
impôrt		import
imposəbl		impossible
impresiv		impressive

▶ **NOTE:** The word beginning *im-* is expressed by the *m* stroke.

32-D. THE WORD BEGINNING *ELECTR-* AND THE COMPOUND ELEMENT *ELECTRIC*

Sound(s) of	Shorthand Stroke(s)	Longhand Word(s)
ilektr-, ilektrik	(disjoined)	electric
ilektrisətē		electricity
ilektrəfəkāshən		electrification
ilektroniks		electronics

▶ **NOTE:** The word beginning *electr-* and the compound element *electric* are expressed by a disjoined combination of the *e* and *l* strokes placed above the line of writing.

New words: _____ rural _____ history _____ reality _____ modern _____ educational _____ familiar _____ brochure _____ extended

32-E. THE WORD ENDINGS *-TITUDE,* *-TITUTE,-TUDE*

Sound(s) of	Shorthand Stroke(s)	Longhand Word(s)
-tətüd,-tətüt, -tüd	(disjoined)	
altətüd		altitude
instətüt		institute
magnətüd		magnitude
substətüt		substitute

▶ **NOTE:** A disjoined combination of the *t* and *u* strokes represents the word endings *-titude,* *-titute,-tude.*

New words: _____ safety _____ southern _____ substitution _____ institutions _____ level _____ heavy _____ advancement _____ don't _____ potential _____ foreign

LESSON 32

Page 95

Griffin, tracer, into the, status, arrived, morning's, recheck, progress, unfortunately, rejected, replacement, shipped, via, Continental, freight, hardened, and are, undergoing, final, machining, you will find, eminently

52-D-5. TRANSCRIPTION TIPS

52-D-3. SPELLING

52-D-4. VOCABULARY PREVIEW OF NEW MATERIAL

LESSON 52

Page 152

32-F. GEOGRAPHICAL LOCATIONS

tn	Knoxville, Tennessee (TN)
ne	Omaha, Nebraska (NE)
fl	Tampa, Florida (FL)

NOTE: In proper names, -ville is written *v*.

New words: respectively, suitable, Ford, Dr. (CF)

32-G. REINFORCEMENT

New words: United, hotel, processing, pleasant, age, cancellation, profitable, we'll, widely, summer, attached, discoveries

32-H. PRECISION PRACTICE

32-I. PREPARATION FOR LESSON 33

Continue the usual pattern of study, using 32-A and 32-G for "double thought" phrase writing.

LESSON 32

The current manual, which I prepared, needs revision.
The manual that is currently being used needs revision.

▶ NOTE: In the following paragraph, Rules 3-6 will need to be applied as well as the one above.

52-D. PREPARATION FOR LESSON 53

As you prepare for Lesson 53, follow the same procedures as for similar exercises in previous lessons.

52-D-1. PUNCTUATION

Rule 7. Use a comma to separate a nonrestrictive phrase or clause from the rest of the sentence. Restrictive phrases or clauses are not separated from the rest of the sentence because they are essential to the meaning of the sentence.

52-D-2. WORD SELECTION

device—a plan, contrivance, or invention
devise—to plan, to contrive, or to invent

▶ NOTE: The following material includes words presented in Lessons 48-51 as well as those above.

LESSON 33

33-A. RECAP OF LESSON 32

New phrases: to facilitate to call about this

New words: legislation(CF) populated Senate speed Congress appointment sugar rescue act export methods cotton held

33-B. LONG I LOOK ALIKES

If a word contains the phonetic *iə* and the outline could be mistaken for another word, then it is written with a dot inside the *i* stroke.

Sound(s) of	Shorthand Stroke(s)	Longhand Word(s)
īə		
līən		lion
kwīət		quiet
sīəns		science

NOTE: The dot distinguishes the above words from *line*, *quite*, and *signs*.

New words: favorable loans distribution longer

LESSON 33 — Page 97

LESSON 52

52-A. THE TEN-WORD SPRINT

52-B. PREVIEWED NEW DICTATION

The new dictation contains the words and phrases you previewed in 51-D-4.

52-C-1. THE 100-WORD DASH

52-C-2. THE 200-WORD DASH

(4) [shorthand]

33-C. THE WORD ENDING -INGLY

Sound(s) of	Shorthand Stroke(s)	Longhand Word(s)
-inglē	___ (disjoined)	
inkrēsinglē		increasingly
sēminglē		seemingly

▸ NOTE: The word ending *-ingly* is expressed by a disjoined combination of the *ng* stroke and the *-ly* loop.

New words: confirmed, predict, research, unfortunately, trust, neglected, peers, guarantee, willingly, models, accordingly

(1) [shorthand]
(2) [shorthand]
(3) [shorthand]

33-D. THE WORD BEGINNINGS SUPER-, SUPR-

Sound(s) of	Shorthand Stroke(s)	Longhand Word(s)
səpr-, süpr-	(disjoined)	
süprintendnt		superintendent
səpirēər		superior
süpərvīzərē		supervisory
səprēm		supreme

▸ NOTE: The word beginnings *super-*, *supr-* are expressed by the *s* stroke written above the line.

New words: telegraph, together, telephone, sample, restoring, east, sacrifice, characteristics (CF), south

(1) [shorthand]
(2) [shorthand]
(3) [shorthand]
(4) [shorthand]
(5) [shorthand]

LESSON 33

Page 98

51-D-4. VOCABULARY PREVIEW OF NEW MATERIAL

Fleming, occasion, anniversary, friendship, to thank you for your, loyalty, location, steady, associations, prosperity, continuous, energy, quarters, eventful, dedication, bronze, faith, pioneer, memorializing, statue, enabled, landmark, garden, settlers

51-D-3. SPELLING

51-D-5. TRANSCRIPTION TIPS

LESSON 51   **Page 149**

33-E. GEOGRAPHICAL LOCATIONS

shorthand al — Mobile, Alabama (AL)

shorthand oh — Springfield, Ohio (OH)

shorthand ok — Tulsa, Oklahoma (OK)

NOTE: In proper names, *-field* is written *f*.

New words: *shorthand* black *shorthand* via *shorthand* white

(1) *shorthand outline*

(2) *shorthand outline*

33-F. THE WORD ENDINGS -ALOGY, -OLOGY

Sound(s) of	Shorthand Stroke(s)	Longhand Word(s)
-ələjē, -olələjē	*o* (disjoined)	
ənalələjē	*shorthand*	analogy
sīkolələjē	*shorthand*	psychology
teknolələjē	*shorthand*	technology

NOTE: The word endings *-alogy, -ology* are expressed by a disjoined *o* stroke.

New phrases: *shorthand* is this *shorthand* if you have

New words: *shorthand* evidence *shorthand* psychologic *shorthand* approach *shorthand* psychologists *shorthand* attendance *shorthand* technological *shorthand* storm *shorthand* psychological

(1) *shorthand*

(2) *shorthand*

(3) *shorthand*

(4) *shorthand*

(5) *shorthand*

33-G. REINFORCEMENT

New words: *shorthand* capital (capitol) *shorthand* emerging *shorthand* told

shorthand paragraphs

33-H. PRECISION PRACTICE

shorthand

33-I. PREPARATION FOR LESSON 34

Follow the usual pattern of study, using 33-A and 33-G for "double thought" phrase writing.

LESSON 33   Page 99

51-D. PREPARATION FOR LESSON 52

Continue the same pattern of study for the following exercises that you used for the preceding lesson.

51-D-1. PUNCTUATION

Rule 6. Use a comma to separate words, phrases, or clauses in a series.

The sidewalk sale featured clothing, shoes, accessories, and luggage.

▶ **NOTE:** The following notes require the application of Rules 2-5 as well as the one above.

51-D-2. WORD SELECTION

guarantee—to insure the performance of; an agreement that insures performance, genuineness, reliability
guaranty—an agreement that insures performance, genuineness, reliability

▶ **NOTE:** The notes on the following page include words presented in Lessons 47-50 as well as those above.

LESSON 51   Page 148

LESSON 34

34-A. RECAP OF LESSON 33

New phrases: Respectfully yours (CF)

Dear Sir (CF)   Dear Madam (CF)

New words: arises   Ladies   clergyman   affiliations   establishments   loss   religious   philosophy   express   geographical   average   above   closed   frequently   cent   undertook   observe   failure   night   retail

34-B. GEOGRAPHICAL LOCATIONS

New Orleans, Louisiana (LA)

Toledo, Ohio (OH)

Wilmington, Delaware (DE)

New words: normal   postage   duplicate   dividend (CF)   spent   daily   that's

LESSON 34   Page 100

LESSON 51

● **51-A. THE TEN-WORD SPRINT**

● **51-B. PREVIEWED NEW DICTATION**

You will take dictation that includes the words previewed in 50-D-4.

● **51-C-1. THE 100-WORD DASH**

● **51-C-2. THE 200-WORD DASH**

34-C. VOCABULARY EXPANSION

New phrases: ⟡ you'll be ⟡ and is

New words: ⟡ proud ⟡ confidence ⟡ warehouse ⟡ fiscal ⟡ far ⟡ welcome ⟡ volume ⟡ plastic ⟡ prior ⟡ pipe ⟡ privilege ⟡ professional ⟡ guide ⟡ theory

New words: ⟡ catalog ⟡ colors ⟡ yesterday ⟡ carbon ⟡ clean ⟡ invoice ⟡ inches ⟡ came ⟡ below

LESSON 34 Page 101

50-D-2. WORD SELECTION

it's—the contraction for "it is"
its—of or belonging to it

NOTE: The following notes include words shown in 46-C-2, 47-D-2, 48-D-2, and 49-D-2 as well as those above.

50-D-3. SPELLING

50-D-4. VOCABULARY PREVIEW OF NEW MATERIAL

Bowman, quotations, residence, Forest, Boulevard, remove, away, premises, stucco, exposed, sheathing, covered, buff-colored, asbestos, panel, whitepine, lumber, strips, one of the, constitute

50-D-5. TRANSCRIPTION TIPS

New words: regional, sincere, enrollments, civil, duplicate (v), initial, greatest, health, Harry, commitment, felt, term, proof, vital, commerce

34-D. PRECISION PRACTICE

34-E. PREPARATION FOR LESSON 35

Follow the usual pattern of study. Read each plate in Lesson 34; write the preview outlines 3 consecutive times; then write 34-A in "double thought" phrases.

Write each of the following outlines 3 consecutive times. They will appear in new matter dictation in Lesson 35.

New phrases: about your (about you), may not, I am sure

New words: carry, peace (piece), fire, life, payroll, zero, remain, dipping, rest, table, death, chart, double, indemnity, words, red (read), code, net, spend, consult, else, neither, underselling, nor, overselling, latter, bad, former

LESSON 34 — Page 102

50-D. PREPARATION FOR LESSON 51

Again, follow the procedure for the similar exercises in previous lessons.

50-D-1. PUNCTUATION

Rule 5. In a compound sentence, use a semicolon between clauses that are joined by a conjunctive adverb, such as *so, therefore, hence, yet, however, otherwise, still,* and *furthermore.*

The court awarded damages to the plaintiff; however, an appeal will probably be made in the near future.

> **NOTE:** The following notes require application of Rules 1-4 as well as the one above.

LESSON 35

35-A. RECAP OF LESSONS 27-33

New phrase: to keep

New words: cooperate, touch, obligation, practices, pens, reasonable, quarterly, signature, easiest, status, completion, entrusting, selection, risk, leave

LESSON 50

50-A. THE TEN-WORD SPRINT

50-B. PREVIEWED NEW DICTATION

New material previewed in 49-D-4 will be dictated to you.

50-C-1. THE 100-WORD DASH

50-C-2. THE 200-WORD DASH

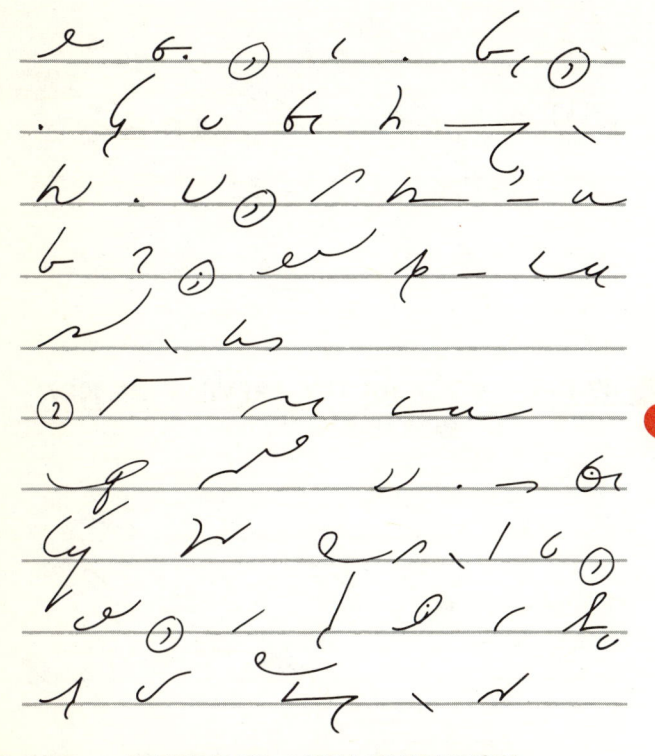

35-B. PREVIEWED NEW DICTATION

Your teacher will dictate new material containing outlines practiced in 34-E.

35-C. GEOGRAPHICAL LOCATIONS

Paris, France

Tokyo, Japan

Toronto, Canada

New words: typist   fraction   extremely   pounds   gross

35-D. VOCABULARY EXPANSION

New phrases: to speak   I would be

New words: lessons   film   declared   admission   participation   junior   season   competency   feet   trainee   glad   behalf   foot   fit

LESSON 35 — Page 104

49-D-2. WORD SELECTION

later—after a lapse of time
latter—the last named of two or more things or persons

NOTE: The following notes include words given in 46-C-2, 47-D-2, and 48-D-2 as well as those given above.

49-D-3. SPELLING

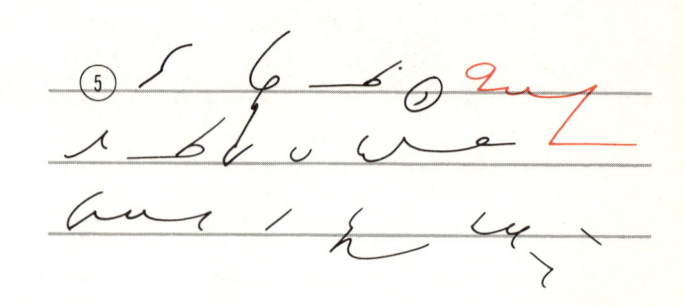

49-D-4. VOCABULARY PREVIEW OF NEW MATERIAL

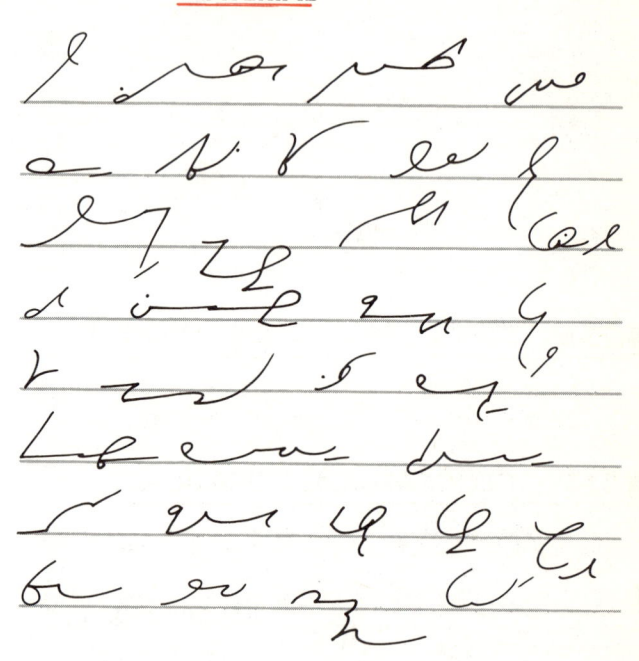

today's, headlines, dramatic, story, America, defending, freedom, wherever, it has been, challenged, inflation, domestic, priorities, etc., homemaker, economists, probability, further, inasmuch, whether, Elks, gymnasium, Eleanor, Fowler, intimate (adj.), equals, crisis, presentation, representatives, panel, we know, unusual, printed

49-D-5. TRANSCRIPTION TIPS

LESSON 49   Page 143

New phrase: _____ to produce

New words: _____ child _____ wire _____ Assurance _____ fountain _____ off _____ suspects (n) _____ Title _____ fence _____ children _____ Mart _____ Abstract _____ reply _____ parent _____ whose _____ formal _____ Trade _____ portion _____ attorney _____ front

New words: _____ directive _____ phrases _____ communications _____ kindest _____ scientific _____ reference _____ violations _____ trite

35-E. PREPARATION FOR LESSON 36

Write twice the outlines that appear in theory exercises in the first 34 lessons.

Write each preview outline in this lesson 3 consecutive times. Read the plates so that you can take the material from dictation at gradually increasing rates. Remember, you can write shorthand as fast as you can think it!

LESSON 35

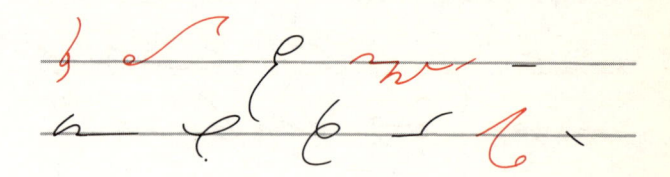

49-D. PREPARATION FOR LESSON 50

For each of the exercises follow the same procedures that you followed in Lessons 47 and 48.

49-D-1. PUNCTUATION

Rule 4. Use a semicolon between coordinate clauses that are joined by a pure conjunction when either or both of the clauses contain a comma.

If you want a human relations expert, I can recommend Dr. Ward; but, if you want an accounting expert, I would suggest Dr. Pearce.

NOTE: The paragraph below requires application of Rules 1-3 as well as the one above.

LESSON 36

36-A. SPEED BUILDER

You will take from dictation at increasing rates the material given in the plates in Lesson 35. This practice will help automize recall and thus speed recording.

36-B. PREPARATION FOR LESSON 37

Now that you have completed all the theory, you will be studying two aspects of shorthand skill development: (1) increasing speed of recall of outlines that have already been presented and (2) broadening your shorthand vocabulary to include new outlines. You will also be reviewing English fundamentals which are essential to accurate transcription.

Each exercise has a specific purpose; keep it in mind as you follow the suggested procedures.

36-B-1. THEORY MASTERY

Write each outline in the lists 3 consecutive times, saying the word as you write it. Read the plate notes; then write the plate material in "single thought" phrases.

36-B-2. SPEED ACCELERATOR

In the plate below, 51 Speedforms or Speedform related words appear. Read the material; then write the shorthand outlines in "double thought" phrases so that you will be able to take the material from dictation at high speed in the next session.

LESSON 36 Page 106

48-D-5. TRANSCRIPTION TIPS

LESSON 49

49-A. THE TEN-WORD SPRINT

49-B. PREVIEWED NEW DICTATION

Your teacher will dictate to you new material that you previewed in 48-D-4.

49-C-1. THE 100-WORD DASH

49-C-2. THE 200-WORD DASH

LESSON 49   Page 141

36-B-3. GEOGRAPHICAL LOCATIONS

Berlin, Germany

Cairo, Egypt

London, England

36-B-4. VOCABULARY PREVIEW OF NEW MATERIAL

Write each outline 3 consecutive times, saying the word or phrase as you write it. The new dictation material in 37-B contains these words and phrases.

Russell, Graham, intelligent, textbooks, variety, publishers, accomplishment, pressure, peak, truly, understandable, occasional, misrouted, carrier, intent, distant, Rochester, strong, wishful, is to be, genuine, overhauled, streamlined, lowest, level, we will see, to it, must have, Adam, Crawford, jet, busy, on us, incidentally, September, October, July, August.

36-B-5. PRECISION PRACTICE

Write the color outlines twice; then write the entire material once, paying particular attention to proportion.

LESSON 36

48-D-2. WORD SELECTION

their—of or belonging to them
there—in or at that place; used to introduce a sentence or clause

▶ NOTE: The following notes include words presented in 46-C-2 and 47-D-2 as well as those given above.

48-D-3. SPELLING

48-D-4. VOCABULARY PREVIEW OF NEW MATERIAL

something, mighty, don't, I've, internal, auditor, familiar, loyal, that's, Hopkins, dividend (CF), share, easier, manufacturers, cooperate, outstanding, liberal, installment, plus, until, genuinely, lovely, mahogany, master, bedroom, suites, queen-size, we've, shipment, imported, accent, patio, garden

LESSON 48

LESSON 37

37-A. PHRASE EMPHASIS

These notes contain 21 common phrases. Read the notes; then your teacher will dictate the material to you at high speed.

37-B. PREVIEWED NEW DICTATION

Your teacher will dictate new material containing outlines you practiced in 36-B-4.

37-C. READING-RECORDING FLUENCY

Read the plate notes silently or in unison, as directed by your teacher. The outlines in color represent words or phrases that are either new or need extra writing to ensure fluency in recording.

New word: congressmen

LESSON 37 — Page 108

48-C-2. THE 200-WORD DASH

48-D. PREPARATION FOR LESSON 49

Follow the same procedure you did for Lesson 48.

48-D-1. PUNCTUATION AND WRITING NUMBERS

Rule 3. Definite numbers over ten are written in figures. Numbers from one to ten inclusive are written as words. Always spell out a number that begins a sentence. Amounts of money and percentages are expressed in figures whether they are above or below ten and whether they are definite or approximate. Even amounts of money are written without the decimal and ciphers; amounts below $1 are written as a figure and are followed by the word "cent" or "cents" as appropriate.

The Payroll Department asked for 11 new machines.
Forty baggage cars were destroyed by the collision.
This week Hazel earned $100, which represented an increase of 10 cents an hour or 4 percent.

NOTE: The paragraph on the following page reviews Rules 1 and 2 as well as the one given here.

37-D. PREPARATION FOR LESSON 38

The following exercises are similar to the ones appearing in Lesson 36; use the same directions.

37-D-1. THEORY MASTERY

mm, mn, -ment:

-ble, -bility:

sh, -sion, -tion:

37-D-2. SPEED ACCELERATOR

Included in the notes are 29 Speedforms or Speedform related words.

37-D-3. GEOGRAPHICAL LOCATIONS

Write each geographical location two times; then write the plate notes in "double thought" phrases.

Brussels, Belgium

Melbourne, Australia

Vienna, Austria

LESSON 37

Page 109

LESSON 48

48-A. THE TEN-WORD SPRINT

Follow the same procedure as for the similar exercise 47-A.

48-B. PREVIEWED NEW DICTATION

Again, your teacher will dictate new material that you have previewed.

48-C-1. THE 100-WORD DASH

LESSON 48 Page 138

37-D-4. VOCABULARY PREVIEW OF NEW MATERIAL

hello, personally, isn't, acquainted, Merit, publications, chat, mutual, I'll be, Statler, Washington, Booksellers, greetings, popular, wholesome, beautifully, to tell, colorful, compilation, timely, spiritual, reproductions, magnificent (CF), illustrated (CF), poems, characteristic (CF), Christmas, about these, some of our, salesmen

37-D-5. PRECISION PRACTICE

LESSON 38

38-A. PHRASE EMPHASIS

There are 20 phrases in the following plate notes.

38-B. PREVIEWED NEW DICTATION

The new material containing the outlines you practiced in 37-D-4 will be dictated to you.

38-C. READING-RECORDING FLUENCY

Follow the same procedure as for 37-C, page 108.

47-D-2. WORD SELECTION

affect—to influence, to modify, to assume artificially
effect—an immediate result or general impression; to accomplish or bring about

▶ NOTE: These notes include words used in 46-C-2 as well as those above.

47-D-3. SPELLING

47-D-4. VOCABULARY PREVIEW OF NEW MATERIAL

Oakland, dependent, municipal, university, growth, economically, socially, integral, facilitate, financing, simpler, expedite, courtesy, registered, serial, billfold, purse, recognition (CF), loyalty, integrity, token, appreciation, economic, intellectual, spiritual, welfare, surrounding, communities, browse, furniture, newly, appliance, acquainted

47-D-5. TRANSCRIPTION TIPS

LESSON 47   Page 137

38-D. PREPARATION FOR LESSON 39

Follow the directions that were given in Lesson 36 for similar exercises.

47-C-2. THE 200-WORD DASH

New word: ____ schedule (CF)

47-D. PREPARATION FOR LESSON 48

Follow the same pattern of preparation as for Lesson 46.

47-D-1. PUNCTUATION

Rule 2. Use a comma to separate coordinate clauses joined by one of the pure conjunctions unless the clauses are very short.

What changes in procedures do you think are essential, and how can we make those changes quickly?
He will sign and then he will go.

▶ NOTE: The notes on the following page require application of both Rule 1 and Rule 2.

LESSON 47

38-D-1. THEORY MASTERY

nd, nt, nv:

ind-, int-, inv-:

-ive, -sive, -tive:

be-, de-:

ld:

38-D-2. SPEED ACCELERATOR

Included in the notes are 38 Speedforms or Speedform related words.

38-D-3. GEOGRAPHICAL LOCATIONS

Calcutta, India

Manila, Philippines

Moscow, Russia

38-D-4. VOCABULARY PREVIEW OF NEW MATERIAL

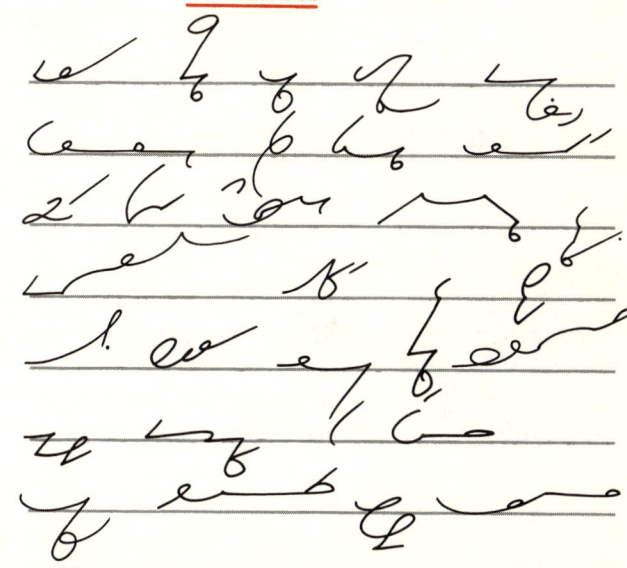

credit, agency, require, automobile, comprehensive, premiums, payable, policy, remitted, second, by that, underwriters, delinquency (CF), succeeding, continental, indicated, signified, assist, checking, avoid, ineligibility, inadvertently (CF), incorrect, communicate, promptly, will find, terminate, representation, let me

38-D-5. PRECISION PRACTICE

LESSON 38

Page 112

LESSON 47

47-A. THE TEN-WORD SPRINT

How fast can you write when you have quick recall of the outlines for the words dictated? This exercise will give you some indication.

Familiarize yourself with the shorthand notes. Then your teacher will dictate the sentence to you. Your objective is to write the sentence as many times as you can before time is called.

When time is called, count the number of complete sentences you wrote. Multiply that number of sentences by 10 (the number of standard dictation words in the sentence). Add the number of words you wrote in any partially completed sentence. Multiply the resulting figure by a number designated by your teacher. If she timed you for 12 seconds, she will ask you to multiply by 5, for that would give you your rate for one minute at 100 words per minute.

47-B. PREVIEWED NEW DICTATION

Material you previewed in 46-C-4 will be dictated to you.

47-C-1. THE 100-WORD DASH

Read the notes quickly. Outlines that may need special attention are in color; your teacher may dictate them before giving you the entire 100 standard dictation words.

LESSON 47 Page 135

LESSON 39

39-A. PHRASE EMPHASIS
There are 21 phrases in the notes.

39-B. PREVIEWED NEW DICTATION
The dictation will contain the words and phrases you studied in 38-D-4.

39-C. READING-RECORDING FLUENCY

46-C-3. SPELLING

This exercise will provide practice in spelling correctly certain words that are commonly misspelled in written communications. These "special problem" words appear in color. Check the words in the dictionary to be sure that you are spelling them correctly; then transcribe each sentence. You may need to check some of the other words, too!

46-C-4. VOCABULARY PREVIEW OF NEW MATERIAL

In your notebook write each outline 3 times consecutively.

here's, introduce, juvenile, quarter, handsome, concept, children's, wonderful, surprise, it would be, youngster, birthday, adult, contents, illustrations (CF), introductory, inspiration, heroes, skiing, swimming, mysteries, chemistry, countless, undoubtedly, easier, educational, varied, helpful, privileged, thumb, girls, coin, of them

46-C-5. TRANSCRIPTION TIPS

Be ready to discuss the ideas which are expressed in the notes.

LESSON 46   Page 134

39-D. PREPARATION FOR LESSON 40

Continue the same pattern of study as for Lessons 36-39. Remember your two objectives: (1) to speed the recall of shorthand outlines; (2) to increase the number of words you can write in shorthand.

39-D-1. THEORY MASTERY

ex-:
-ous, -us:
al-:
-ful:

LESSON 46

46-A. PHRASE EMPHASIS

There are 17 phrases in the notes.

If the analysis is correct, we should have no problem handling the current situation.

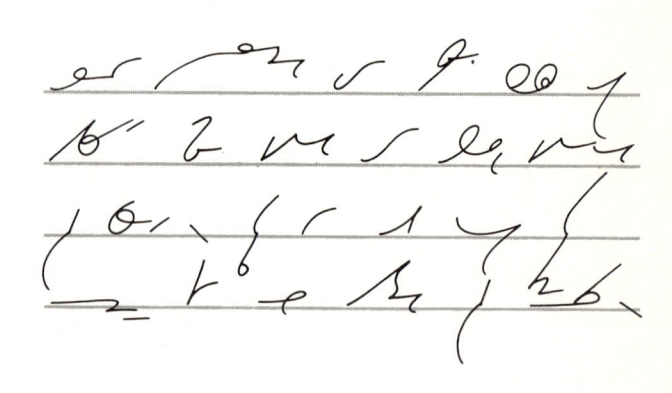

46-B. PREVIEWED NEW DICTATION

Material you previewed in 45-D-4 will be dictated to you.

46-C. PREPARATION FOR LESSON 47

The preparation for the next ten lessons will review basic punctuation rules, word usage, spelling, and word division rules. There will be reviews of skills and knowledges learned in typewriting that are needed for effective transcription. You will continue to expand your shorthand vocabulary and notetaking rate.

46-C-1. PUNCTUATION

Study the rule presented and the example given; then transcribe the paragraph, adding the correct punctuation.

Rule 1. Use a comma to set off a dependent clause that precedes a main clause.

46-C-2. WORD SELECTION

Certain words that are similar in spelling, pronunciation, or meaning may cause difficulty in transcription. A group of commonly confused words is given below; the spellings and definitions will help you differentiate between the words. Study the words carefully; then transcribe the shorthand notes.

to—denotes direction or introduces an infinitive
too—in addition, more than enough, to such a degree
two—the number "2" written out in word form

LESSON 46   Page 133

39-D-2. SPEED ACCELERATOR

There are 56 Speedforms or Speedform related words in the notes.

39-D-3. GEOGRAPHICAL LOCATIONS

Bangkok, Thailand
Saigon, Vietnam
Tehran, Iran

39-D-4. VOCABULARY PREVIEW OF NEW MATERIAL

adhesive, technology, expansion, traditional, glue, rubber, cement, bond, surfaces, plastic, possibilities, vast, scope, tremendously, basically, we must, selection, application, starch-derived, fluid, filmy, thinly, consistency, does not, solvent, primarily, laminating, wood, synthetic, resins, resistant, newest, certainly, potential, concrete, thrive, research, laboratories

39-D-5. PRECISION PRACTICE

LESSON 39 — Page 115

The simultaneous and/or "chaining" of several subskills in the transcription process makes that process a most challenging and fascinating one. As the transcriber looks at her notes and "translates" them into a typed form, she must visualize mentally the typed word for each shorthand outline. She must carry the thought of the sentence so that an outline won't be mistranscribed because of more than one meaning for the outline or because of poor proportion. She must strike a typewriter key for each letter in each word as it is visualized mentally, and she must operate the various machine parts. As she types, she must recognize the sentence structure so that she can bring forth from her "memory bank" the appropriate spelling, punctuation rule, figure typing rule, word division rule, and capitalization rule.

Before she begins transcription, she must select the appropriate stationery and display style for the message. She must keep in mind any special directions she may have been given, such as special notations.

The transcriber must proofread the transcript and correct all errors. In the office situation, she must accept interruptions that break her concentration. The greater skill the transcriber has with the many subskills, the easier will be the integration of them in transcribing.

WORD SELECTION

Phonetic Studies

colon

it's—the contraction for "it is"
its—of or belonging to it

Will they break the law as they brake to a stop?

Quotation Marks.

SPELLING RULES

Use a comma to set off a dependent clause that precedes a main clause.

Capitalize the first word and all important words in titles of books, periodicals and articles.

beach — beech

heard—herd

Divide words only between syllables.

I before e
Except after c
Or when sounded like a
As in neighbor and weigh.

Hyphenate

Spelling

I merely wanted to collate the pages of the memorandum.

Word Division Rules

Punctuation

well-mannered

LESSON 40

40-A. PHRASE EMPHASIS

There are 20 phrases in the notes.

40-B. PREVIEWED NEW DICTATION

The dictation will contain the words that you studied in 39-D-4.

40-C. READING-RECORDING FLUENCY

LESSON 40

Page 116

com-:
long i
look alikes:

45-D-3. GEOGRAPHICAL LOCATIONS

Akron, Ohio (OH)
Albany, New York (NY)
Memphis, Tennessee (TN)

45-D-4. VOCABULARY PREVIEW OF NEW MATERIAL

45-D-2. SPEED ACCELERATOR

The notes contain 40 Speedforms or Speedform related words.

recorder, you haven't, used, Redwood, issued, wondering, purchases, when you are, away, truly, conserves, cash, permanent, expenses, taxes, monthly, enables, to buy, frequent, user, traveling, pleasure, forward, remove, worry, vacations

45-D-5. PRECISION PRACTICE

LESSON 45

New word: negotiations (CF)

40-D. PREPARATION FOR LESSON 41

Follow the same directions as for Lessons 36-40.

40-D-1. THEORY MASTERY

con-:
dm, dn:
dd, dt, td:
in-:
-er, -or:

40-D-2. SPEED ACCELERATOR

The notes contain 38 Speedforms or Speedform related words.

45-C. READING-RECORDING FLUENCY

45-D. PREPARATION FOR LESSON 46

Follow the same pattern of study as for Lessons 36-44.

45-D-1. THEORY MASTERY

sub-:

-alogy, -ology:

electric, electr-:

inter-, intr-:

long i with basic vowel:

-gram, -graph:

-ject:

LESSON 45   Page 130

40-D-3. GEOGRAPHICAL LOCATIONS

Buenos Aires, Argentina
Lima, Peru
Rio de Janeiro, Brazil

40-D-4. VOCABULARY PREVIEW OF NEW MATERIAL

cash, daytime, version, sensational, TV, network, golf, a.m., Eastern, Standard, presently, popular, quiz, deluxe, giant, refrigerator, antique, copper, unique, kitchen, showcase, Pacific, Industries, camera, closeups, flashed, strong, exclusive, literally, millions, household, audiences, watching, stations, viewers, bid, they will be, into your, to find, authorized, winners, publicity, reflected, entries, needless, nationwide, promotional, venture

40-D-5. PRECISION PRACTICE

LESSON 40 — Page 118

44-D-4. VOCABULARY PREVIEW OF NEW MATERIAL

Phillips, aptitude, surely, educational, brochure, intensive, project, seminar, experiment, launched, edition, we wanted, absolutely, families, intellectual, cultural, degrees, aside, horizons, amateur, she could, acquire, lectures, museum, portfolio, if this, to instruct, orientation, fundamental, concepts

44-D-5. PRECISION PRACTICE

LESSON 45

45-A. PHRASE EMPHASIS

There are 29 phrases in the notes.

45-B. PREVIEWED NEW DICTATION

Your teacher will dictate to you new material; it contains the words and phrases you studied in 44-D-4.

LESSON 45 — Page 129

LESSON 41

41-A. PHRASE EMPHASIS

There are 25 phrases in the notes.

41-B. PREVIEWED NEW DICTATION

The dictation will contain words and phrases you studied in 40-D-4.

41-C. READING-RECORDING FLUENCY

Page 119

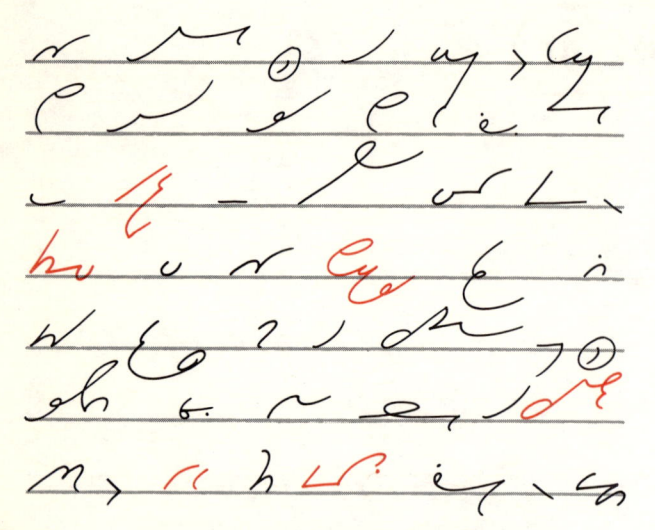

44-D. PREPARATION FOR LESSON 45

As you follow your usual pattern of study, make a conscious effort to expand your shorthand vocabulary and increase your speed of recall.

44-D-1. THEORY MASTERY

super-, supr-:

self:

-scribe, -script:

-hood, -ward:

-titude, -titute, -tude:

-ed:

per-, pur-:

under:

44-D-2. SPEED ACCELERATOR

The notes contain 47 Speedforms or Speedform related words.

44-D-3. GEOGRAPHICAL LOCATIONS

Anchorage, Alaska (AK)

Colorado Springs, Colorado (CO)

Wheeling, West Virginia (WV)

LESSON 44
Page 128

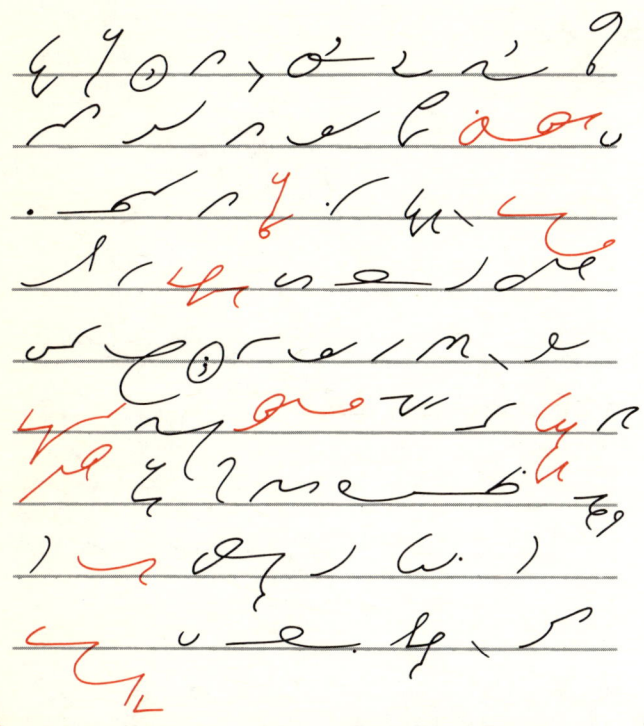

41-D. PREPARATION FOR LESSON 42

Continue the same pattern of study that you have followed in preparing for Lessons 36-41. Always keep in mind the purposes of vocabulary expansion and automatic recall.

41-D-1. THEORY MASTERY

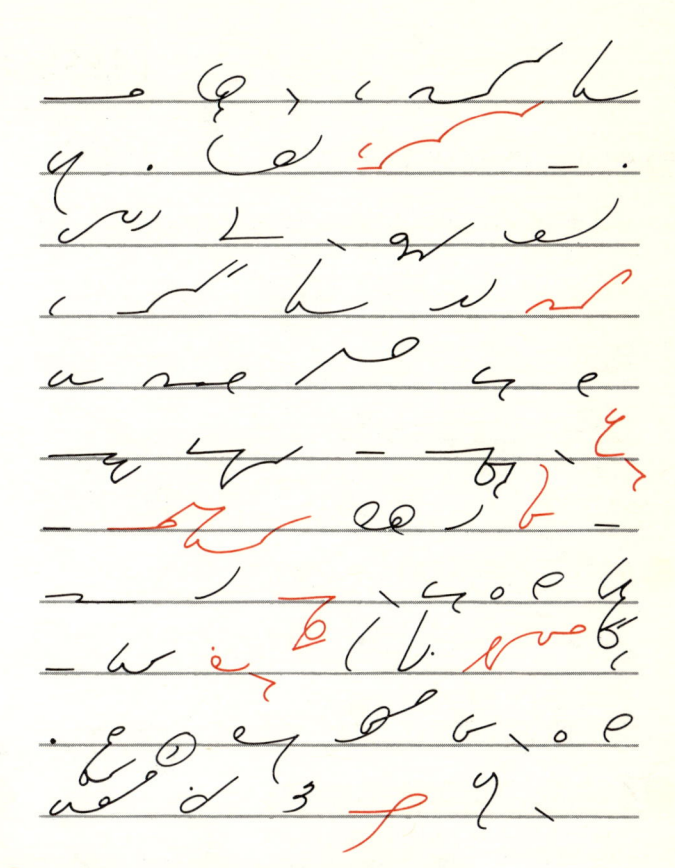

41-D-2. SPEED ACCELERATOR

There are 24 Speedforms or Speedform related words in the notes.

41-D-3. GEOGRAPHICAL LOCATIONS

Hartford, Connecticut (CT)

Miami, Florida (FL)

Providence, Rhode Island (RI)

LESSON 41 — Page 120

LESSON 44

44-A. PHRASE EMPHASIS

There are 30 phrases in the notes.

44-B. PREVIEWED NEW DICTATION

Your teacher will dictate material containing words and phrases previewed in 43-D-4.

44-C. READING-RECORDING FLUENCY

41-D-4. VOCABULARY PREVIEW OF NEW MATERIAL

Bennett, Wear's, Calendar, January, delighted, to its, subscribers, constant, retailers, clothing, to promote, useful, smart, keen, assortment, specific, practical, pictures, example, fathers, reprints, ads, punch, interpretation, consumer, regulations, analysis, specialty, semiannual, interruption, I've, described, modest, don't, merchant, clipped, scientific, OK (okay), subscription

41-D-5. PRECISION PRACTICE

LESSON 42

42-A. PHRASE EMPHASIS

There are 21 phrases in the notes.

42-B. PREVIEWED NEW DICTATION

Material you previewed in 41-D-4 will be dictated to you.

42-C. READING-RECORDING FLUENCY

43-D-3. GEOGRAPHICAL LOCATIONS

Bakersfield, California (CA)
Bridgeport, Connecticut (CT)
St. Petersburg, Florida (FL)

New words: objective; recognition (CF)

43-D-4. VOCABULARY PREVIEW OF NEW MATERIAL

Wheeler, becoming, increasingly, serious, eventually, headquarters (CF), administration, issued, bulletins, outwitting, passers, pamphlet, contained, pointers, significant (CF), location, signature, examination, worthless, nonlocal, drawn, identification, customer's, accuracy, if it's, postdated, more than, to be sure, branch, numerical, written, legibility, legibly, ink, erasures, payee, two-party, exact, depending, average, beyond, salesclerk

43-D-5. PRECISION PRACTICE

42-D. PREPARATION FOR LESSON 43

Follow the same pattern of study as for Lessons 36-42.

42-D-1. THEORY MASTERY

th,-ther,-thor:

-tual:

-ing:

-acle,-ical,-icle:

-ingly:

oi,oy,ou,ow:

y:

43-D. PREPARATION FOR LESSON 44

Once again follow the same pattern of study as for Lessons 36-43.

43-D-1. THEORY MASTERY

-sation,-zation:

over:

tran-,trans-:

-ship:

-ulate:

ng,nk:

-casion,-cation:

43-D-2. SPEED ACCELERATOR

The notes contain 59 Speedforms or Speedform related words.

LESSON 43

Page 125

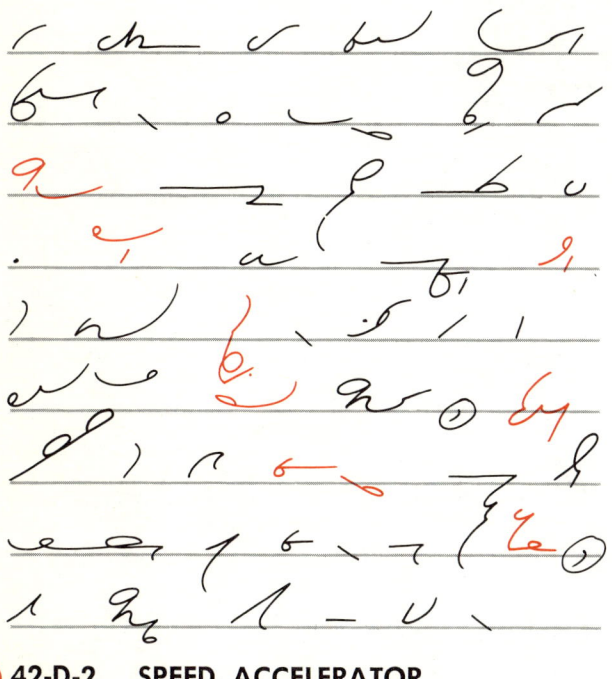

42-D-2. SPEED ACCELERATOR

The notes contain 44 Speedforms or Speedform related words.

42-D-3. GEOGRAPHICAL LOCATIONS

Las Vegas, Nevada (NV)
Louisville, Kentucky (KY)
New Haven, Connecticut (CT)

42-D-4. VOCABULARY PREVIEW OF NEW MATERIAL

comment, listen, another, pertinent, carpet, you may not, maintenance, maintained, wood, flooring, selected, you may be, enthusiastic (CF), remarks, Northwest, Lumber, Metals, several, thousand, poorly, he would have, mountain, moth, proofers, Liberty, Conditioner, dirty, headaches, shrinkage, musty, dampness, adjacent, exclusively, protective, imperative, longevity, thoroughly, acquainted, economies, let's, partnership, economical

42-D-5. PRECISION PRACTICE

LESSON 42

LESSON 43

43-A. PHRASE EMPHASIS

There are 23 phrases in the notes.

43-B. PREVIEWED NEW DICTATION

Material you previewed in 42-D-4 will be dictated to you.

43-C. READING-RECORDING FLUENCY

1500 MOST-USED WORDS

A, 1-C
Ability, 29-B
Able, 1-C
About, 9-C
Above, 34-A
Accept, 3-C
Accepted, 6-C
Accident, 23-B
Accordance, 6-B
According, 7-D
Accordingly, 33-C
Account, 21-B
Accounting, 22-A
Accounts, 22-B
Acknowledge, 31-C
Act, 33-A
Action, 15-A
Active, 18-B
Activities, 19-A
Activity, 18-B
Actual, 26-E
Actually, 26-E
Add, 18-B
Added, 10-B
Addition, 7-C
Additional, 7-C
Address, 21-B
Addressed, 23-F
Adequate, 25-D
Administration, 15-A
Advance, 6-B
Advantage, 14-E
Advantages, 16-B
Advertising, 7-D
Advice, 2-C
Advise, 2-C
Advised, 6-C
Advising, 7-D
Affairs, 17-D
After, 3-C
Again, 21-E
Against, 22-A
Age, 32-G
Agencies, 29-A
Agency, 28-B
Agent, 25-A
Agents, 24-A
Ago, 27-A
Agree, 17-A
Agreed, 25-A
Agreement, 18-D
Agricultural, 21-A
Ahead, 14-C
Aid, 15-B
Air, 6-C
All, 6-C
Allow, 28-B
Almost, 21-C
Along, 15-D
Already, 21-C
Also, 21-D
Although, 21-C
Always, 21-C
Am, 10-C
Amended, 32-E
Amendment, 32-A
Among, 15-E
Amount, 10-D
Amounts, 34-B
An, 1-C
Analysis, 30-G
And, 5-D
Announced, 19-B
Annual, 21-D
Another, 19-D
Answer, 5-D
Anxious, 15-D

Any, 3-D
Anything, 18-D
Appear, 29-D
Appears, 30-G
Application, 30-G
Applications, 25-G
Applied, 13-D
Apply, 33-C
Appointment, 33-A
Appreciate, 10-D
Appreciated, 11-A
Appreciation, 25-A
Appropriate, 30-G
Approval, 25-G
Approved, 28-B
Approximately, 15-E
Are, 1-E
Area, 25-A
Areas, 26-A
Around, 17-C
Arrange, 11-D
Arrangement, 30-H
Arrangements, 19-D
Arrive, 30-G
Article, 24-B
Articles, 24-B
As, 1-C
Ask, 6-B
Asked, 12-C
Asking, 9-A
Assist, 9-B
Assistance, 24-F
Assistant, 17-B
Associates, 1-E
Association, 7-C
Associations, 27-A
Assume, 26-B
Assure, 10-A
Assured, 28-B
At, 1-E
Attached, 32-G
Attend, 24-G
Attendance, 33-F
Attention, 17-B
Authority, 30-E
Authorized, 29-D
Automobile, 26-D
Available, 22-E
Average, 34-A
Aware, 31-E
Away, 13-D
Back, 9-C
Background, 33-F
Bad, 34-E
Balance, 19-D
Bank, 15-D
Banking, 31-B
Banks, 17-A
Base, 29-A
Based, 34-C
Basic, 26-A
Basis, 9-C
Be, 9-C
Because, 13-C
Become, 23-A
Been, 9-C
Before, 22-B
Begin, 30-D
Beginning, 30-B
Behalf, 35-D
Being, 14-E
Believe, 9-C
Below, 34-C
Benefit, 30-C
Benefits, 34-C
Best, 9-C
Better, 9-C

Between, 23-A
Beyond, 24-C
Big, 11-D
Bill, 9-C
Billing, 34-C
Bills, 22-E
Black, 33-E
Blank, 16-C
Board, 9-C
Bond, 10-B
Bonds, 9-C
Book, 9-C
Booklet, 18-D
Books, 11-D
Both, 21-A
Box, 19-B
Boxes, 24-E
Boys, 19-C
Branch, 14-C
Bring, 15-C
Brochure, 32-D
Brought, 30-E
Budget, 28-B
Build, 22-F
Building, 25-B
Built, 25-B
Bulletin, 17-B
Bureau, 24-C
Business, 9-C
But, 9-C
Buy, 12-A
Buying, 9-C
By, 9-C
Call, 33-A
Called, 17-C
Calling, 28-B
Calls, 17-B
Game, 34-C
Campaign, 28-B
Can, 3-B
Cancellation, 32-G
Cannot, 3-E
Capacity, 26-D
Capital, 33-G
Car, 3-B
Carbon, 34-C
Card, 35-A
Cards, 6-C
Care, 3-B
Carefully, 27-A
Carried, 35-D
Carry, 34-E
Case, 3-D
Cases, 21-A
Cash, 7-B
Catalog, 34-C
Cause, 23-D
Cent, 34-A
Center, 25-E
Central, 9-B
Cents, 19-E
Certain, 29-A
Certainly, 34-E
Certificate, 9-B
Certified, 13-A
Chairman, 11-C
Chance, 14-C
Change, 11-C
Changed, 11-C
Changes, 13-A
Chapter, 27-D
Charge, 21-A
Charged, 21-E
Charges, 32-A
Check, 12-C
Checked, 11-C
Checking, 11-D

Checks, 35-A
Chief, 25-A
Children, 35-D
Choice, 29-D
Church, 30-A
Circumstances, 28-B
Cities, 22-D
Citizens, 21-A
City, 3-E
Civil, 34-C
Claim, 29-A
Claims, 28-B
Class, 34-C
Classes, 24-D
Clean, 34-D
Clear, 7-D
Close, 35-A
Closed, 34-A
Club, 30-E
Code, 34-E
Collect, 30-F
Collection, 23-A
College, 18-B
Color, 34-C
Colors, 34-C
Come, 10-C
Comes, 35-B
Coming, 14-C
Comments, 25-G
Commerce, 34-C
Commercial, 22-D
Commission, 34-B
Commitment, 34-C
Committee, 10-D
Community, 26-D
Companies, 31-A
Company, 10-D
Complete, 22-D
Completed, 35-B
Completely, 34-A
Completion, 35-A
Concern, 25-G
Concerned, 25-E
Concerning, 28-B
Condition, 3-E
Conditions, 5-C
Conference, 22-C
Confidence, 34-C
Confirm, 34-C
Congratulations, 31-D
Congress, 33-A
Connection, 26-C
Consider, 6-B
Considerable, 28-B
Consideration, 7-C
Considered, 6-C
Construction, 7-C
Consumer, 22-C
Contact, 9-B
Contained, 18-A
Continue, 22-C
Continued, 27-E
Continuing, 31-A
Contract, 9-B
Contracts, 11-A
Contribution, 17-B
Control, 9-B
Convenience, 6-A
Convenient, 5-D
Convention, 9-B
Conversation, 32-B
Cooperate, 35-A
Cooperation, 32-A
Cooperative, 26-B
Copies, 27-E
Copy, 10-D
Corporation, 30-A

Correct, 5-D
Correspondence, 6-B
Cost, 6-C
Costs, 9-A
Cotton, 33-A
Could, 6-A
Council, 22-A
Country, 27-E
County, 24-G
Course, 10-A
Courses, 7-D
Court, 30-G
Cover, 13-C
Coverage, 30-A
Covered, 21-E
Covering, 31-E
Covers, 31-C
Credit, 19-A
Cross, 31-C
Current, 25-A
Currently, 32-B
Customer, 25-A
Customers, 24-A
Cut, 35-B
Daily, 34-B
Damage, 32-A
Data, 19-A
Date, 5-D
Dated, 35-A
Dates, 6-C
Day, 3-E
Days, 3-E
Deal, 17-A
Dealer, 9-B
Dealers, 11-C
Death, 34-E
Decide, 32-A
Decided, 21-A
Decision, 10-A
Defense, 6-C
Delay, 3-E
Delivered, 6-C
Delivery, 24-F
Demand, 23-D
Demonstration, 31-F
Department, 11-C
Departments, 17-C
Deposit, 35-A
Described, 27-E
Description, 28-C
Design, 6-C
Designed, 35-B
Desire, 3-E
Desired, 34-C
Desk, 5-C
Detail, 19-A
Detailed, 20-B
Details, 18-C
Determine, 22-A
Determined, 35-A
Develop, 6-B
Developed, 6-C
Development, 17-C
Did, 18-C
Difference, 35-B
Different, 27-B
Difficult, 6-C
Dinner, 30-B
Direct, 3-E
Directly, 15-A
Director, 23-E
Directors, 23-G
Discount, 25-G
Discuss, 3-E
Discussed, 6-C
Discussion, 17-A
Display, 21-A

Appendix

i

Distribution, 33-B
District, 32-A
Dividend, 34-B
Division, 7-C
Do, 3-E
Doctor, 33-F
Does, 11-D
Doing, 28-B
Dollar, 4-C
Dollars, 3-E
Don't, 32-E
Done, 21-D
Double, 34-E
Doubt, 21-C
Down, 9-B
Dozen, 7-B
Drainage, 32-B
Drive, 9-C
Drop, 24-C
Due, 3-E
Duplicate, 34-B
During, 9-B
Duty, 32-A
Each, 11-C
Earliest, 29-D
Early, 13-C
Earnings, 25-E
Easily, 13-C
East, 33-D
Easy, 1-E
Economic, 18-D
Economy, 18-D
Education, 18-B
Educational, 32-D
Effect, 3-C
Effective, 26-C
Effort, 10-C
Efforts, 10-D
Eight, 19-E
Either, 19-D
Election, 14-C
Electric, 32-D
Eligible, 30-E
Else, 34-E
Emergency, 31-D
Employee, 34-C
Employees, 26-F
Employment, 19-D
Enable, 28-B
Enclose, 5-D
Enclosed, 6-C
Enclosing, 7-D
End, 5-D
Endorsement, 27-C
Engineering, 25-B
Enjoy, 21-A
Enjoyed, 22-A
Enough, 9-B
Entire, 29-D
Entirely, 13-C
Entitled, 27-D
Envelope, 5-D
Equipment, 14-E
Error, 21-B
Especially, 19-B
Established, 27-D
Estate, 27-A
Estimated, 35-A
Even, 3-D
Evening, 19-E
Event, 5-D
Ever, 2-D
Every, 2-D
Everyone, 12-A
Everything, 18-D
Evidence, 33-F
Examination, 17-D
Example, 17-D
Excellent, 17-D
Except, 17-D
Excess, 32-A

Exchange, 27-E
Executive, 26-B
Existing, 35-A
Expect, 17-D
Expected, 19-A
Expense, 17-D
Expenses, 18-A
Experience, 17-D
Experienced, 24-A
Explain, 17-D
Explained, 20-B
Export, 33-A
Express, 34-A
Extend, 33-A
Extended, 32-D
Extension, 30-A
Extent, 22-A
Extra, 28-B
Extremely, 35-C
Face, 11-A
Facilities, 26-F
Fact, 3-C
Factory, 6-C
Facts, 3-C
Faculty, 29-D
Fair, 7-B
Fall, 14-E
Familiar, 32-D
Family, 13-C
Far, 34-C
Farm, 24-D
Fast, 30-G
Favor, 6-B
Favorable, 33-B
Feature, 23-C
Features, 23-C
Federal, 25-E
Fee, 32-A
Feel, 3-C
Fees, 30-E
Feet, 35-D
Felt, 34-C
Few, 3-C
Field, 24-D
Figure, 18-B
Figures, 20-B
File, 35-D
Filed, 35-A
Files, 3-C
Filing, 22-F
Fill, 28-B
Film, 35-D
Final, 5-C
Finance, 35-A
Financial, 30-A
Financing, 32-B
Find, 5-D
Fine, 3-D
Finest, 30-B
Finish, 21-C
Fire, 34-E
Firm, 18-D
Firms, 18-D
First, 14-E
Fiscal, 34-C
Fit, 35-D
Five, 8-C
Floor, 15-E
Folders, 22-F
Follow, 6-C
Following, 11-D
Follows, 35-D
Food, 21-E
Foot, 35-D
For, 10-C
Force, 29-A
Foreign, 32-E
Form, 10-C
Formal, 35-D
Forms, 10-D
Forth, 23-A

Forward, 30-E
Forwarded, 35-B
Found, 9-B
Four, 8-C
Fourth, 30-D
Free, 10-B
Freight, 10-B
Friend, 10-B
Friends, 10-B
From, 10-C
Front, 35-D
Full, 27-E
Fully, 25-G
Fund, 19-E
Funds, 21-D
Furnish, 34-C
Furnished, 29-E
Furniture, 23-C
Further, 23-B
Future, 23-D
Gas, 28-B
Gave, 11-D
General, 19-E
Generally, 35-A
Get, 13-A
Getting, 29-A
Give, 14-C
Given, 17-A
Gives, 15-A
Giving, 19-F
Glad, 35-D
Go, 11-D
Going, 11-D
Good, 11-D
Goods, 15-A
Got, 31-B
Government, 13-E
Grade, 15-B
Graduate, 15-B
Great, 15-B
Greater, 23-E
Greatest, 34-C
Greatly, 20-B
Green, 28-B
Gross, 35-C
Group, 15-B
Groups, 29-C
Growing, 25-A
Growth, 28-A
Guarantee, 33-C
Guide, 34-C
Had, 11-C
Half, 31-B
Hand, 15-A
Handle, 29-D
Handled, 24-A
Handling, 25-A
Hands, 29-D
Happy, 25-A
Hard, 28-C
Has, 11-C
Have, 2-D
Having, 7-D
He, 1-C
Head, 11-D
Health, 34-C
Hear, 11-C
Heard, 28-B
Hearing, 15-B
Heavy, 32-E
Held, 33-B
Help, 11-D
Helpful, 25-G
Helping, 13-B
Her, 2-D
Here, 11-D
Herewith, 35-D
Hesitate, 29-D
High, 11-D
Higher, 31-B
Highly, 18-B

Highway, 32-A
Him, 11-D
His, 1-C
History, 32-D
Hold, 29-D
Home, 27-A
Hope, 10-D
Hospital, 15-E
Hospitals, 33-A
Hotel, 32-G
Hour, 1-E
Hours, 2-B
House, 19-E
Housing, 17-C
How, 17-C
However, 17-C
I, 1-B
I'm, 29-E
Idea, 23-G
Ideas, 28-B
If, 3-C
Immediate, 14-E
Immediately, 14-E
Importance, 14-E
Important, 14-E
Improve, 15-E
Improved, 24-C
Improvement, 19-A
In, 3-D
Inch, 35-D
Inches, 34-C
Include, 35-D
Included, 23-H
Includes, 35-B
Including, 31-C
Income, 17-C
Increase, 18-B
Increased, 26-A
Increases, 34-C
Increasing, 13-C
Indeed, 5-D
Indicate, 30-D
Indicated, 21-A
Individual, 5-D
Industrial, 30-B
Industries, 6-A
Industry, 5-D
Inform, 35-D
Information, 10-B
Informed, 13-C
Initial, 34-C
Inquiry, 30-D
Inspection, 31-G
Instead, 29-D
Institute, 32-E
Institutions, 32-E
Instructions, 13-F
Insurance, 30-A
Insured, 28-B
Interest, 18-D
Interested, 31-A
Interesting, 23-H
Interests, 27-A
International, 18-D
Into, 5-D
Inventory, 22-G
Investment, 13-E
Invitation, 5-D
Invite, 5-D
Invited, 10-D
Invoice, 34-C
Invoices, 35-C
Involved, 30-H
Is, 1-C
It, 1-D
It's, 32-B
Item, 17-B
Items, 18-D

Its, 13-C
Itself, 31-B
Job, 11-D
Jobs, 13-D
Join, 19-C
Junior, 35-D
Just, 11-D
Keep, 13-D
Keeping, 34-B
Kind, 5-D
Kindest, 35-D
Kindly, 35-D
Know, 3-D
Knowledge, 18-A
Known, 11-C
Labor, 21-A
Laboratory, 21-A
Land, 32-A
Large, 21-A
Larger, 28-A
Largest, 30-B
Last, 9-A
Late, 2-D
Later, 5-D
Latest, 7-D
Latter, 34-E
Law, 32-A
Learn, 32-D
Lease, 2-D
Least, 28-B
Leave, 35-A
Left, 9-C
Legal, 30-A
Legislation, 33-A
Length, 15-D
Less, 26-A
Let, 24-A
Letter, 2-D
Letters, 2-D
Level, 32-E
Liability, 29-B
License, 31-B
Life, 35-D
Light, 5-D
Like, 3-B
Limited, 29-C
Line, 30-H
Lines, 9-A
List, 3-D
Listed, 20-B
Lists, 21-D
Literature, 29-B
Little, 3-C
Live, 30-C
Living, 22-A
Loan, 35-B
Loans, 33-B
Local, 27-E
Located, 25-G
Location, 25-C
Long, 15-C
Longer, 33-B
Look, 5-D
Looking, 23-A
Loss, 34-A
Lot, 5-B
Lots, 5-C
Low, 35-B
Lower, 22-G
Machine, 31-B
Machines, 31-E
Made, 10-C
Magazine, 27-C
Mail, 27-C
Mailed, 31-B
Mailing, 34-B
Main, 21-A
Maintain, 35-A
Maintenance, 31-B
Major, 15-B
Make, 10-C

Appendix

ii

Makes, 30-A
Making, 10-C
Man, 11-D
Management, 13-E
Manager, 19-A
Managers, 15-B
Manner, 31-D
Manual, 23-G
Manufacture, 13-D
Manufacturers, 29-A
Manufacturing, 17-D
Many, 13-D
Market, 25-A
Marketing, 34-C
Material, 10-C
Materials, 12-B
Matter, 23-D
Matters, 23-G
Maximum, 30-H
May, 10-C
Me, 10-D
Mean, 35-A
Means, 15-E
Medical, 24-B
Meet, 18-B
Meeting, 11-D
Meetings, 25-E
Member, 35-A
Members, 13-D
Membership, 30-B
Men, 13-D
Mentioned, 19-A
Merchandise, 11-C
Method, 35-A
Methods, 33-A
Might, 23-G
Military, 28-B
Million, 19-E
Mind, 26-B
Minimum, 28-B
Minute, 35-B
Minutes, 18-D
Miss, 21-D
Model, 34-C
Models, 33-C
Modern, 32-D
Money, 13-D
Month, 13-D
Monthly, 27-E
Months, 13-E
More, 10-C
Morning, 22-A
Mortgage, 13-F
Most, 19-F
Motor, 28-C
Move, 22-A
Moving, 22-A
Much, 14-E
Must, 10-C
Mutual, 26-E
My, 10-C
Name, 21-E
Names, 18-B
Nation, 18-A
National, 35-A
Nature, 30-D
Near, 27-A
Necessary, 3-D
Need, 3-E
Needed, 8-B
Needs, 4-C
Net, 34-E
Never, 28-B
New, 3-D
News, 15-E
Newspaper, 15-E
Next, 9-B
Night, 34-A
No, 3-E
Nor, 34-E
Normal, 34-B

North, 33-G
Not, 3-D
Note, 34-C
Noted, 33-G
Nothing, 18-D
Notice, 9-B
Now, 18-A
Number, 10-D
Numbers, 13-B
Obligation, 35-A
Obtain, 19-F
Obtained, 22-A
Of, 2-D
Off, 35-D
Offer, 10-B
Offered, 29-A
Offering, 10-B
Office, 5-C
Officer, 11-C
Officers, 9-B
Offices, 9-B
Official, 28-B
Often, 21-A
Oil, 19-C
Old, 22-F
On, 3-D
Once, 27-D
One, 3-D
Only, 13-C
Open, 19-D
Operate, 35-A
Operating, 30-B
Operation, 13-C
Operations, 24-F
Opinion, 24-C
Opportunities, 18-B
Opportunity, 14-E
Or, 3-E
Order, 3-E
Ordered, 6-C
Orders, 3-E
Organization, 11-D
Organizations, 23-G
Original, 22-A
Other, 19-D
Others, 31-D
Otherwise, 19-D
Our, 1-E
Out, 17-C
Outline, 35-B
Outside, 35-D
Outstanding, 18-D
Over, 21-B
Own, 5-D
Owner, 5-D
Owners, 29-A
Package, 34-C
Page, 35-D
Pages, 31-C
Paid, 30-E
Paper, 11-D
Papers, 13-F
Paragraph, 31-C
Part, 11-C
Participate, 32-A
Participation, 35-D
Particular, 15-E
Particularly, 15-E
Parts, 25-A
Pass, 29-D
Passed, 35-A
Past, 27-C
Pay, 10-D
Payable, 22-E
Paying, 10-D
Payment, 16-A
Payments, 13-F
Payroll, 34-E
Pays, 35-B
Peace, 34-E
People, 10-D

Per, 28-B
Percent, 19-E
Percentage, 27-B
Performance, 26-F
Perhaps, 23-A
Period, 19-A
Permit, 18-B
Person, 18-B
Personal, 18-D
Personally, 27-C
Personnel, 19-A
Persons, 18-B
Phone, 35-A
Physical, 28-B
Picture, 26-A
Piece, 35-C
Pieces, 35-D
Pipe, 34-C
Place, 15-B
Placed, 11-C
Plan, 10-D
Planning, 28-B
Plans, 10-D
Plant, 20-B
Plastic, 34-C
Pleasant, 32-G
Please, 10-D
Pleased, 11-D
Pleasure, 15-A
Plus, 29-C
Point, 33-D
Points, 21-E
Policies, 30-A
Policy, 35-B
Portion, 35-D
Position, 24-A
Positions, 35-D
Possibility, 31-G
Possible, 26-A
Possibly, 23-A
Post, 27-E
Postage, 34-B
Potential, 32-E
Pound, 35-C
Pounds, 35-C
Power, 17-C
Practical, 24-B
Practice, 35-C
Prefer, 18-B
Premium, 35-B
Premiums, 30-A
Preparation, 27-B
Prepared, 19-A
Present, 18-B
Presented, 32-E
Presently, 34-B
President, 23-B
Press, 19-B
Previous, 29-C
Previously, 29-D
Price, 28-B
Prices, 15-A
Principal, 29-D
Printed, 11-D
Printing, 24-A
Prior, 34-C
Private, 30-E
Privilege, 34-C
Probably, 25-A
Problem, 18-B
Problems, 19-A
Procedure, 21-E
Procedures, 19-A
Proceed, 32-B
Process, 34-C
Processing, 32-G
Produce, 35-D
Product, 18-B
Production, 29-A
Products, 18-B
Professional, 34-C

Profit, 34-C
Profitable, 32-G
Profits, 30-A
Program, 31-C
Programs, 33-D
Progress, 29-A
Project, 30-D
Projects, 31-C
Promotion, 35-A
Prompt, 18-B
Promptly, 19-F
Proof, 34-C
Proper, 21-C
Properly, 23-A
Property, 27-A
Proposal, 28-B
Proposed, 29-D
Protection, 26-D
Proud, 34-C
Prove, 32-A
Provide, 18-B
Provided, 19-F
Provides, 19-F
Providing, 25-B
Provisions, 31-C
Public, 11-A
Publication, 25-C
Published, 23-H
Purchase, 23-H
Purchased, 34-C
Purchasing, 35-B
Purpose, 18-B
Purposes, 19-A
Put, 18-D
Qualified, 32-A
Quality, 3-B
Quantity, 6-C
Quarterly, 35-A
Question, 3-B
Questions, 3-B
Quickly, 30-D
Quite, 31-F
Quote, 32-A
Radio, 31-F
Range, 35-D
Rate, 1-E
Rates, 1-E
Rather, 29-D
Reach, 28-B
Reached, 23-F
Read, 9-C
Reading, 24-D
Ready, 5-C
Real, 9-C
Realize, 24-F
Really, 34-A
Reason, 29-D
Reasonable, 35-A
Reasons, 21-E
Receipt, 7-A
Receive, 1-E
Received, 6-C
Receiving, 7-D
Recent, 15-B
Recently, 29-D
Recommend, 34-C
Recommendations, 29-D
Recommended, 26-E
Record, 3-E
Records, 3-E
Red, 34-E
Reduced, 32-C
Refer, 20-B
Reference, 35-D
Referred, 17-D
Regard, 15-B
Regarding, 15-B
Regards, 35-D
Regional, 34-C
Regret, 15-B
Regular, 11-D

Regulation, 31-D
Regulations, 31-E
Relations, 25-A
Relative, 26-B
Release, 30-A
Remain, 34-E
Remember, 22-G
Rent, 35-B
Rental, 32-A
Repair, 33-A
Replacement, 31-D
Reply, 35-D
Report, 14-E
Reported, 28-A
Reports, 15-A
Representative, 26-B
Representatives, 26-F
Request, 3-B
Requested, 6-C
Requesting, 7-D
Requests, 3-E
Require, 5-E
Required, 14-C
Requirements, 13-E
Requires, 12-A
Research, 33-C
Reservations, 12-B
Reserve, 3-E
Respect, 15-E
Response, 5-E
Responsibility, 29-B
Responsible, 31-B
Rest, 34-E
Result, 5-E
Results, 5-E
Retail, 34-A
Return, 1-E
Returned, 6-C
Returning, 7-D
Revenue, 30-A
Review, 26-E
Right, 1-E
Risk, 35-A
Road, 24-G
Room, 19-D
Route, 24-G
Rules, 3-A
Run, 31-D
Running, 35-A
Safety, 32-E
Said, 6-A
Salary, 29-C
Sale, 2-D
Sales, 3-D
Same, 23-A
Sample, 33-D
Samples, 34-C
Satisfactory, 1-D
Satisfied, 6-C
Save, 2-C
Saving, 11-D
Savings, 29-C
Say, 1-B
Schedule, 28-B
Scheduled, 32-B
School, 5-D
Schools, 5-D
Season, 35-D
Second, 31-C
Secretarial, 29-C
Secretary, 3-D
Section, 23-G
Secure, 34-C
Security, 26-D
See, 1-B
Seeing, 7-D
Seem, 18-B
Seems, 27-E
Seen, 24-B
Select, 15-B
Selected, 31-C

Appendix

iii

Selection, 35-A	Soon, 5-C	Taken, 11-A	Traffic, 24-G	Way, 3-E
Self, 31-B	Sorry, 22-A	Taking, 18-A	Training, 35-D	Ways, 11-D
Sell, 18-B	Sound, 24-B	Talk, 11-D	Transfer, 30-G	We, 2-C
Selling, 9-A	Source, 28-B	Tax, 23-A	Transportation, 30-G	We'll, 32-G
Semester, 29-D	South, 33-D	Taxes, 23-A	Travel, 18-A	Weather, 32-A
Senate, 33-A	Southern, 32-E	Teacher, 23-C	Treasury, 29-A	Week, 5-D
Send, 3-D	Space, 19-D	Teachers, 24-A	Tremendous, 29-C	Weekly, 13-C
Sending, 7-D	Special, 13-F	Teaching, 34-C	Trial, 31-D	Weeks, 9-C
Sent, 5-D	Specific, 15-E	Technical, 31-D	Trip, 13-C	Weight, 4-B
Separate, 31-A	Specifications, 31-A	Telephone, 33-D	Trouble, 22-B	Welcome, 34-C
Series, 26-A	Specified, 21-E	Television, 7-C	Truck, 35-D	Well, 2-D
Serve, 2-C	Speed, 33-A	Tell, 3-D	Trucks, 28-B	Were, 7-D
Served, 6-C	Spring, 15-C	Temporary, 29-A	True, 2-B	West, 32-A
Service, 3-A	Staff, 10-A	Ten, 12-A	Trust, 33-C	Western, 28-B
Services, 8-B	Stand, 17-B	Term, 34-C	Try, 2-A	What, 2-C
Serving, 7-D	Standard, 31-C	Terms, 35-C	Trying, 35-A	Whatever, 8-C
Session, 15-D	Start, 7-C	Territory, 5-E	Turn, 27-A	When, 5-D
Set, 13-D	State, 1-D	Test, 35-D	Twelve, 31-C	Where, 2-C
Sets, 35-B	Stated, 6-C	Than, 3-D	Twenty, 19-E	Whether, 21-D
Seven, 32-G	Statement, 13-E	Thank, 14-E	Two, 1-D	Which, 11-C
Several, 5-C	States, 1-D	Thanking, 35-A	Type, 29-A	While, 2-D
Shall, 7-B	Station, 7-C	Thanks, 34-A	Types, 34-C	White, 33-E
Share, 7-B	Status, 35-A	That, 2-B	Typing, 35-D	Who, 11-D
Shares, 35-B	Steel, 24-E	That's, 34-B	Unable, 28-B	Whole, 32-A
She, 29-C	Step, 15-A	The, 2-D	Under, 14-D	Whom, 11-D
Sheet, 31-D	Still, 29-A	Their, 2-B	Understand, 24-D	Whose, 35-D
Sheets, 7-B	Stock, 5-D	Them, 10-C	Understanding, 26-A	Why, 2-C
Ship, 7-B	Stocks, 5-D	Then, 3-D	Unfortunately, 33-C	Wide, 35-D
Shipment, 25-F	Stop, 28-B	There, 2-B	Union, 30-C	Will, 2-D
Shipments, 28-C	Storage, 22-F	Therefore, 31-F	Unit, 28-B	Willing, 7-D
Shipped, 28-C	Store, 1-E	These, 2-B	United, 32-G	Wire, 35-D
Shipping, 7-D	Stores, 7-D	They, 2-B	Units, 28-B	Wish, 7-B
Shop, 29-C	Story, 15-E	Thing, 18-D	University, 27-A	Wishes, 7-B
Short, 7-B	Street, 5-D	Things, 25-E	Unless, 19-B	With, 2-C
Shortly, 34-C	Student, 23-B	Think, 14-E	Until, 19-B	Within, 31-G
Should, 7-B	Students, 23-D	Thinking, 35-B	Up, 15-B	Without, 25-A
Show, 7-B	Studies, 32-C	Third, 7-C	Upon, 23-G	Women, 28-B
Showing, 20-B	Study, 18-C	Thirty, 19-E	Urge, 29-D	Won't, 28-B
Shown, 7-B	Style, 6-C	This, 3-D	Us, 6-A	Word, 35-D
Shows, 31-F	Subject, 30-D	Those, 5-B	Use, 1-D	Words, 34-E
Side, 35-D	Submit, 27-B	Though, 6-C	Used, 14-B	Work, 3-B
Sign, 12-A	Submitted, 34-C	Thought, 3-D	Useful, 25-B	Worked, 6-C
Signature, 35-A	Subscription, 27-C	Thousands, 31-F	Using, 7-D	Workers, 24-C
Signed, 35-A	Substantial, 27-B	Three, 9-C	Usually, 33-F	Working, 10-B
Similar, 27-A	Success, 3-B	Through, 2-B	Vacation, 25-C	Works, 35-A
Simple, 34-C	Successful, 25-B	Throughout, 17-C	Valuable, 22-B	World, 22-F
Simply, 13-C	Such, 14-E	Thus, 28-B	Value, 9-B	Worth, 2-D
Since, 7-D	Sufficient, 26-D	Time, 17-B	Various, 29-D	Would, 3-E
Sincere, 34-C	Sugar, 33-A	Times, 34-C	Very, 2-D	Write, 1-E
Sincerely, 13-C	Suggest, 11-D	Tire, 3-B	Via, 33-E	Writing, 28-D
Single, 21-D	Suggested, 13-A	Title, 35-D	Vice, 29-D	Written, 17-B
Situation, 14-E	Suggestion, 17-A	To, 1-D	View, 34-A	Wrote, 7-D
Six, 14-C	Suggestions, 20-B	Today, 18-C	Visit, 7-C	Year, 24-C
Size, 5-A	Summer, 32-G	Together, 33-D	Volume, 34-C	Years, 27-D
Sizes, 21-E	Supplies, 17-B	Told, 33-G	Vote, 2-C	Yes, 24-C
Small, 29-C	Supply, 20-A	Too, 1-D	Wage, 23-D	Yet, 24-C
So, 2-A	Support, 13-C	Top, 31-D	Want, 5-D	You, 1-B
Society, 26-D	Sure, 7-B	Total, 19-E	Wanted, 6-C	You'll, 34-C
Sold, 28-A	Survey, 28-B	Touch, 35-A	War, 9-C	Young, 24-C
Solution, 11-A	System, 22-F	Toward, 28-B	Warehouse, 34-C	Your, 1-C
Some, 10-C	Table, 04-D	Town, 28-B	Was, 2-C	Yours, 2-B
Something, 18-D	Take, 3-B	Trade, 35-D	Water, 32-B	Yourself, 31-B
Somewhat, 35-B				

The 1500 Most-Used Words are compiled from two doctoral studies: "The Basic Vocabulary of Written Business Communications," by James E. Silverthorn and "An Analytical Comparison of the Relative Word-Combination Frequencies of Business Correspondence with Phrase Frequencies of Selected Shorthand Textbooks," by Devern J. Perry.

Appendix